Operations Research for Library and Information Professionals

OPERATIONS RESEARCH FOR LIBRARY AND INFORMATION PROFESSIONALS

Dariush Alimohammadi
Department of Library and Information Studies
Tarbiat Moallem University
Tehran
Iran

Ess Ess Publications
New Delhi

Operations Research for Library and Information Professionals

ISBN: 978-81-7000-622-0

Rs.325/-

First Published 2010

Published by:
Ess Ess Publications
4837/24, Ansari Road,
Darya Ganj,
New Delhi-110 002.
INDIA
Phones: 23260807, 41563444
Fax: 41563334
E-mail: info@essessreference.com
www.essessreference.com

Cover Design by *Patch Creative Unit*

Printed and bound in India at Salasar Imaging Systems.

Contents

Table of Notations

In the table of notations, the most popular mathematical symbols used through the text have been defined according to their presence at the book.

Symbol	*Name*	*Meaning*
$=$	Equality	$x = y$ means x and y represent the same thing or value.
$\{ , \}$	set brackets	$\{a,b,c\}$ means the set consisting of a, b, and c.
:	extends; over	$K : F$ means the field K extends the field F.
$<$	is less than	$x < y$ means x is less than y.
$\leq$	is less than or equal to	$x \leq y$ means x is less than or equal to y.
$>$	is greater than	$x > y$ means x is greater than y.
$\geq$	is greater than or equal to	$x \geq y$ means x is greater than or equal to y.
( )	parentheses	Perform the operations inside the parentheses first.
Ø	the empty set	© means the set with no elements.
$\cup$	the union of	$A \cup B$ means the set of those elements which are either in A, or in B, or in both.

$\cap$	intersected with	$A \cap B$ means the set that contains all those elements that A and B have in common.
$-$	negative; minus; the opposite of	-3 means the negative of the number 3.
$\times$	the Cartesian product of ... and ...; the direct product of ... and ...	$X \times Y$ means the set of all ordered pairs with the first element of each pair selected from X and the second element selected from Y.
$\Rightarrow$	implies; if ... then*B*	$A \Rightarrow B$ means if A is true then is also true; if A is false then nothing is said about B.
$\mid$	conditional probability	$P(A \mid B)$ means the probability of the event a occurring given that b occurs.
Σ	sum over ... from ... to ... of	$\sum_{k=1}^{n} a_k$ means $a_1 + a_2 + \ldots + a_n$.
[ ]	1 if true, 0 otherwise	[*S*] maps a true statement S to 1 and a false statement S to 0.
∞	Infinity	∞ is an element of the extended number line that is greater than all real numbers; it often occurs in limits.
Δ	delta; change in	Δx means a (non-infinitesimal) change in x.

2 Preface

2.1 ABOUT THIS BOOK

During the past decades, especially after the World War II, the Operations Research (hereafter will be called OR) has played an important role in economic and social development of countries. From the early days, OR, considered utilizing mathematical models to solve military problems (Kraft and Boyce, 1991; Rowley and Rowley, 1981). Gradually, success in OR projects encouraged professionals from other disciplines to use its techniques and tools in their own fields. Library and Information Sciences / Studies (LIS) was one of the domains affected by the OR and used it severely. Historically, the application of OR in libraries was started in the 1960s and peaked in the early 1970s (Kraft and Boyce, 1991; Ma, 1997; Reisman and Xu, 1994)[1]. While Leimkuhler says that libraries have been more useful to OR than has OR been useful to libraries (1972), Warwick and Bell (2009) consider academic libraries as the main organizations interested in OR application. The environment within which academic libraries now operate is dominated by two features. The first is the requirement for libraries to operate within strict resource constraints and the second is the pace of change brought about by developments in information technology (Warwick, 2009).

This book is in fact an effort to inject OR in LIS, in a manner that it could be used by academic librarians. It has

1. For a derailed history of operations research in libraries refer to Kraft and Boyce (1991).

a systematic structure through which understanding basics of the OR would be possible for librarians, especially those who don't have sufficient knowledge and experience in mathematics. At first, OR is defined and its evolution is illustrated. Then, OR methodology is introduced and its characteristics are discussed. The most important techniques of the OR have been argued throughout the book from absolute to probabilistic and mixed models.

It should be noted that the structure of the book has been borrowed from some of the OR textbooks. Nevertheless, there are little works in the area of mathematics with this general approach to the OR. Most of them trace one of the techniques of OR; for example, linear programming. Therefore, the main feature of the present work is that it has an overview on the OR and tries to support discussions with real examples from the field of LIS. While examples have been provided everywhere to simplify the matter; the last section has specifically been dedicated to a more explanation of the areas of OR application in the field of library and information services.

2.2 HEY, LIBRARIANS, YOU NEED THIS BOOK!

You, all librarians, need this book seriously. First of all, you have to be familiar with the OR as a mathematical approach for handling the daily issues. As human beings, we have a general side of life like others. In this side, we should know how we could adopt mathematical approach and utilize modeling and formulae in the process of decision making. Shopping and transportation are instances of using the mathematics in daily life. At the other hand, as LIS professionals, we have to be acquainted with the areas of LIS that are susceptible for mathematical modeling using OR. Studying this book is also recommended to librarians because there is not any other text in information field with the approach the present work has adopted. The previous works mainly consider application of a technique from the OR (e.g., transportation) in a library operation (e.g., library management).

3 OR Generalities

3.1. OR DEFINITION

Operations Research (OR) is the application of scientific methods and techniques to decision-making (Ma, 1997; Operations research, 1994; Rowley and Rowley, 1981; Ven et al, 2008) and sociotechnical problems (Kraft and Boyce, 1991; Leimkuhler, 1972). A decision-making problem occurs where there are two or more alternative courses of action, each of which leads to a different and sometimes unknown end result (Calderhead, 1997; Nkereuwem and Eteng, 1994; Operations research, 1994). It is also used to maximize the utility of limited resources (Ma, 1997). The objective is to select the best alternative, that is, the one leading to the best result (Lesso, 2007; Operations research, 1994). According to the other definition, OR is used to study the function or operations of an organization so as to develop better ways of planning and controlling changes (Leimkuhler, 1977). Calderhead also provides a definition of the OR implying that it is a research methodology whose main goal is the scientific ordering of meaningful data (1997).

To put these definitions into perspective, the following analogy might be used. In mathematics, when solving a set of simultaneous linear equations, one states that if there are seven unknowns, there must be seven equations. If they are independent and consistent and if it exists, a unique solution to the problem is found. In operations research there may be figuratively "seven unknowns and four equations". There may be a solution space with many feasible solutions which satisfy the equations. Operations research is concerned with establishing the best solution. To do so, some measure of merit and some objective function must be prescribed.

3.2 OR SCOPE

However, some of the researchers look at the OR as a branch of management, engineering, or science, or as a special combination of the three (Leimkuhler, 1977). As part of the field of management, its purpose is to assist decision makers in choosing preferred future courses of action by systematically identifying and examining the alternatives which are available to the manager, and by predicting the possible outcomes from such actions (Rowley and Rowley, 1981). As a branch of engineering, operations research is concerned with the analysis and design of systems for automating and augmenting management-type functions, especially those concerned with information processing and control. It is also viewed as a form of applied science, and is closely related to the fields of statistics, computer science, and optimization methods.

There are several terms associated with the subject matter of this program including:

- Decision science;
- Management science;
- Operational research;
- Operations analysis;
- Operations evaluation;

- Policy science;
- Quantitative analysis;
- Quantitative methods;
- System engineering;
- Systems analysis;
- Systems evaluation; and
- Systems research (Kraft and Boyce, 1991; Operations research, 1994).

Rowley and Rowley (1981) have clarified the exact area in which some of these concepts could be studied. While there are subtle differences and distinctions, the terms can be considered nearly synonymous.

In general, the field can be divided into two general areas with regard to methods. These are those that can be termed mathematical programming (Absolute models) and those associated with stochastic processes (Probabilistic models). While computers are heavily used to solve problems, the term programming should not be considered in that sense, but rather in the general sense of organizing and planning. Also, the tools of probability and statistics are used to a considerable extent in working with stochastic processes (Lesso, 2007). According to the approach adopted by the present work, a third category of models could be added to the previous ones. These three models could be enumerated as follows:

1. Absolute models;
2. Probabilistic models; and
3. Mixed models.

3.3 OR EVOLUTION

While almost every art and every science can reach back into antiquity for its roots, operations research can reach back less than a century to find its beginnings. During the World War I, F. W. Lancaster[2] developed models of combat superiority and victory based on relative and effective firepower. Thomas Edison studied antisubmarine warfare, and in 1915 F. Harris derived the first economic order quantity (EOQ) equation for inventory. Starting in 1905 and continuing into the 1920s, A. Erlang studied the flow of calls into a switchboard and formed the basis of what is now known as queueing theory (Lesso, 2007; Taha, 2007).

Empiricists: The formal beginning of operations research was in England during the World War II, where the term was and still is operational research. Early work concerned air and coastal defense. Typical of the research groups formed was "Blackett's Circus". This interdisciplinary group consisted of three physiologists, two math physicists, an astrophysicist, an army officer, one surveyor, one general physicist, and two mathematicians. The basic mode of operation was to observe the problem area, and then call on the expertise of the various disciplines to apply methods from other sciences to solve the particular problem. In retrospect, this was an era of "applied commonsense", and yet it was novel and highly effective (Lesso, 2007).

Pragmatists: Following World War II. Operations research continued to exist mainly in the military area

2. He is differed from F. W. Lancaster, the emeritus professor of the Graduate School of Library and Information Science, University of Illinois, Urbana-Champaign and the specialist in the indexing and evaluation of information systems.

(Leimkuhler, 1972). The operations research groups formed during the war stayed together, and a number of civilian organizations were established. Following their attempts and in attacking the problem of assigning limited resources to almost limitless demands, the technique of linear programming was developed. Perhaps no other method is more closely associated with the field. Its use quickly spread from the military to the industrial area, and a new dimension was added to operations research (Lesso, 2007; Taha, 2007). At the same time, the use of operations research techniques in business, industry, and government grew rapidly in America (Leimkuhler, 1977; Ven et al, 2008). No longer was it simply "observe, analyze, and try". For the first time the field became "scientific". It could now "optimize" the problems.

It was during this time that formal courses in operations research were first offered. It was also during this time that operations research suffered its first lapse. Linear programming soon was looked to as the cure for too many of industry's ills. Unfortunately, industry's problems were not all linear, and "straightening them out" to fit resulted in many aborted projects and reports that were simply shelved instead of implemented. The early 1950s saw a growth in the number of industrial operations research groups; by the end of the decade, many had disappeared.

Theorists: Toward the end of the 1950s a number of highly skilled scientists emerged who made some substantial contributions to the field. Operations research came of age and matured. In fact, the movement was so far advanced toward developing a sound theoretical base that a new problem arose – the practicality gap (Lesso, 2007). Nowadays, OR is identified as an academic discipline; is taught at Master and Ph.D. levels in many universities all over the world; has an strong theoretical basis; provides various and developing tools and techniques; has already gained too much credit; and plays an important role in decision making processes.

3.4 OR METHODOLOGY

An OR study is rooted in *teamwork*, where the OR analysts and the client work side by side. The OR analysts' expertise in modeling must be complemented by the experience and cooperation of the client for whom the study is being carried out (Taha, 2007). As mentioned above, OR today is a maturing science rather than an art. The success of operations research, where there has been success, has been the result of some simply stated rules. One can enumerate rules as follows:

1. Define and formulate the problem;
2. Construct a model of the system;
3. Select a solution technique;
4. Obtain a solution to the problem;
5. Establish controls over the system or validate the model; and
6. Implement the solution.

The first statement of the problem is usually vague, inaccurate, and sometimes not a statement of the problem at all. Rather, it may be a cataloging of observable effects. It is necessary to identify the decision maker, the alternatives, goals, and constraints, and the parameters of the system. In modeling the system, one usually relies on mathematics, although graphical and analog models are also useful. It is important, however, that the model suggest the solution technique, and not the other way around. Forcing a model to fit a preferred technique led to some of the bad operations research of the past. With the first solution obtained, it is often evident that the model and the problem statement must be modified, and the sequence of the problem-model-technique-solution-problem may have to be repeated several times. The controls are established by performing sensitivity analysis on the parameters. This also indicates the areas in which the data-collecting effort should be made. Implementation is perhaps of the least interest to the theorists, but in reality it is the most important step. If direct action is not taken to implement the solution, the whole effort may end as a dust-collecting report on a shelf. Given the natural inclination to resist change, it is necessary to win the support of the people who will use the new system. To do this, several ploys may be used. Make a member of the using group also a member of the research team. This provides liaison and access to needed data. Educate the users about what the system is – not to the extent of making them experts, but to alleviate any fear of the unknown. Perhaps the major limitation to successful use of operations research lies in this phase (Churchman, 1972; Lesso, 2007; Operations research, 1994; Rowley and Rowley, 1981; Taha, 2007).

Rules of operations research can also be summarized as follows:

1. Formulation of the decision problem;
2. Construction of a model of the decision problem;
3. Analysis and design of a system for solving the problem; and
4. Incorporation of the system into the organization.

The total process is a cyclic one, that is, the research team begins with an elementary formulation of the problem and the construction of as simple a model as is possible to capture the essential features. This leads to a solution system that can be used in an experimental way in the organization to see how it affects the original problem situation. This usually leads to a much better clarification of the problem, enrichment of the model, refinement of the system, and a new round of experimentation in the organization. The process is intended to continue in this way to evolve into a fully satisfactory control of the operations under study, and to also lead to higher levels of management decision making. Because of the hierarchical nature of such decision making in an organization, it is possible to begin at various problem situations and arrive at the same level of understanding and control. However, it is usually most effective to begin with isolated problem situations and then work toward their convergence in a more common structure of decision making, rather than to attempt to develop a total management system at the outset (Leimkuhler, 1977). Nevertheless, a model is never fully accepted in operations research circles until it has been justified in a scientific manner. This means listing the assumptions and deductive steps needed to draw relevant conclusions from the model and giving an orderly description of the design and analysis of experiments aimed at testing hypotheses suggested by the model. Also, a good bit of attention may be given to showing how this model differs from and relates to other models reported in the literature (Leimkuhler, 1972).

3.5. OR CHARACTERISTICS

OR, like any other scientific discipline, has characteristics as follows:

1. **OR focuses on the decision making:** Any decision is the result of a selection process between two or more choices. This process is called decision making. From a general point of view, management is equal to decision making. Decision making has four main steps including:

    - Definition of the problem;
    - Determination of solutions;
    - Evaluation of solutions; and
    - Selection of a solution.

2. **OR follows a scientific approach:** Scientific approach or in other words scientific method is a process proposed primarily by Rene Dekart three centuries ago. Scientific approach has six steps including:

    - Definition of the problem;
    - Observation of the system's behavior;
    - Formulating the hypothesis;
    - Experimental testing of the hypothesis; and
    - Approving or rejecting the recommended hypothesis.

    Both focusing on the decision making and following the scientific approach have overlaps.

3. **OR has a systematic view:** A collection of elements collaborating with each other towards a given purpose is called system. By the system we mean an organization, a department, or a problem. Systems

may have several sub-systems. The best situation in which operations research can take place is the systematic overview of the problem in hand from an upper level; i.e. the system level. Simultaneous analysis of inputs, processors, and outputs satisfies an OR project. There are many other elements (intervening variables) which affect the system's performance. Taking into account these elements that mainly came from the environment, is an essential factor in OR success.

4. **OR is an interdisciplinary area:** Modern organizations have complicated problems which could not be solved by simple solutions. Under such a condition, mixed approach would be of interest to leading managers (Leimkuhler, 1972). In this approach following disciplines mainly involve, to name just a few:

    - Communications;
    - Computer science;
    - Economics;
    - Mathematics;
    - Physics;
    - Politics;
    - Psychology; and
    - Sociology.

    Having a good proficiency in these disciplines is necessary for members of OR teams (typically there are at least three members in each team).

5. **OR uses and develops mathematical models:** Model is a sample of reality. Model simplifies the difficulties of the real problem and lets solver govern the process. While iconic (3-dimensional and physical surrogates of the system, such as an automobile maquette) and analog (2-dimensional figures, like an organizational chart) models are available, mathematical models have a greater impact on problem solving. Advantages of the mathematical models include:

   - Usage in too complicated situations;
   - Simulation of the time needed for the operation;
   - Simplicity of modification;
   - Decreasing the cost of operation;
   - Calculating the risk; and
   - Providing a good context for learning.

   There are absolute (linear programming, non-linear programming, transportation, assignment, and network), probabilistic (Markov chains, queueing theory, and decision analysis), and mixed (dynamic programming and simulation) mathematical models in OR.

6. **OR strongly uses computers:** While it is very hard, but the OR can be done manually. In order to make analyses rapidly, computers are used in calculation. Some software packages have yet been developed so far like LINDO. Kraft and Boyce (1991) have provided a comprehensive list of OR software packages.

4 OR Models

4.1 ABSOLUTE MODELS

4.1.1. Linear programming

The most widely used OR model is linear programming (Taha, 2007), which is a technique for finding the best allocation of commonly used resources among the various activities that use those resources (Leimkuhler, 1977); or, the use of limited resources to meet demands for the output of these resources. This type of problem is found mainly in production systems, but is not limited to this area (Lesso, 2007; Operations research, 1994). If the activities use the resources in amount which are proportional to the outputs of the activities, and if the total value of the output is proportional to output of each individual activity, then for a given set of resources, it is possible to find the optimal assignment of resources to activities (Linear programming, 1994).

In the field of LIS, models of this kind have been used for example to find optimal allocation of budgeted funds to the selection and purchase of library journals (Leimkuhler, 1977). As another example, If there are two types of information services, both of which share the same set of resources (e.g., staff time in scanning, indexing, abstracting), and each of them has a different "unit profit", a linear programming problem is used to find out how many services of each type to produce in order to maximize the total profit (Reisman and Xu, 1994).

In general, complication in the environment of organizations makes the decision making very hard. Managers are faced with many limitations in resources, energy, time, manpower, materials, budget, etc. *If* the main aim of all managers is to gain the most amount of profit or maximizing the process, *then* decreasing the amount of or minimizing the costs and resource losing should be an ideal/ optimum point. Using quantitative methods in planning and decision making is increased as factors affecting the process varied. Linear programming is one of the quantitative methods used to optimize the process in a condition in which resources are going to be limited more and more. Linear programming provides a model including an *objective function*, *variables*, and some *constraints*.

Three main steps should be left out in linear programming:

1. The definition of problem should be capable of using linear programming;
2. The problem should be formulated in a mathematical model; and
3. The problem should be solved using a given mathematical technique.

At the same time, every model of linear programming should have three main characteristics as follows:

1. Proportionality: This property requires the contribution of each decision variable in both the objective function and the constraints to be directly proportional to the value of the variable;

2. Additivity: This property requires the total contribution of all the variables in the objective function and in the constraints to be direct sum of the individual contributions of each variable; and

3. Certainty: All the objective and constraint coefficients of the model are deterministic. This means that they are known constants (Taha, 2007).

The general model of linear programming

Every linear programming model has elements as follows (Taha, 2007):

1. Decision variables (mathematical symbols):

In a linear programming model,
n decision variables can be defined as:

X1: activity amount of 1
X2: activity amount of 2
Xj: activity amount of j

.
.
.
.

Xn: activity amount of n
Or
Xj: (j = 1, 2, …, n)

2. Objective function (mathematical linear relationship); and

$$Max\ (Min)\ Z = C1X1 + C2X2 + \ldots + CjXj + \ldots + CnXn$$

Where: Z = the total value of the objective function

The portion of any single activity of j in the objective function is Cj: (j = 1, 2, …, n)

3. Model limitations (linear relationships among variables).

$$a11x1 + a12x2 + \dots + a1jxj + \dots + a1xn \leq b1$$
$$a21x1 + a22x2 + \dots + a2jxj + \dots + a2xn \leq b2$$
$$\vdots$$
$$ai1x1 + ai2x2 + \dots + aijxj + \dots + xn\ ain \leq bi$$
$$\vdots$$
$$am1x1 + am2x2 + \dots + amjxj + \dots + xn\ amn \leq bm$$
$$x1, x2, \dots, xj, \dots, xn \geq 0$$

In this model, limitations can be shown and replaced as $\leq$, $\geq$ or =. The general model of linear programming can be summarized as follows:

$$Max\ (Min)\ Z = C1X1 + C2X2 + \dots + CjXj + \dots + CnXn$$
$$s.t:$$
$$a11x1 + a12x2 + \dots + a1jxj + \dots + a1xn \leq b1$$
$$a21x1 + a22x2 + \dots + a2jxj + \dots + a2xn \leq b2$$
$$\vdots$$
$$ai1x1 + ai2x2 + \dots + aijxj + \dots + xn\ ain \leq bi$$
$$\vdots$$
$$am1x1 + am2x2 + \dots + amjxj + \dots + xn\ amn \leq bm$$
$$x1, x2, \dots, xj, \dots, xn \geq 0$$

As an example, consider an information service that provides two main services – *X* and *Y*. for every unit of *X* it provides, it gets a *$10* contribution profit, and for *Y* it gets a *$15* contribution. How many should they provide of each? Obviously there must be some limitations – on demand and on providing capacity. Suppose they must provide *50* of *X* and *10* of *Y*, while at the other hand the maximum providing are *120* for *X* and *90* for *Y*. unfortunately, they have only *40* total hours of productive capacity per period (e.g., week), and it takes *0.25* hour to make an *X* and *0.4* hour to make an *Y*. What is their optimal strategy? First, the problem must be formally stated: "Given an information service providing two services, the problem is to maximize the contribution to profit, by the choice of how many of each service to provide, subject to limits on demand (upper and lower) and available service hours."

If *X* equals the number of first service provided and *Y* the number of the second service provided, the system can be modeled as follows:

$$\text{Maximize profit contrib.} = 10X + 15Y$$

$$\text{Subject to}$$

$$X \geq 50$$

$$X \leq 120$$

$$Y \geq 10$$

$$Y \leq 90$$

$$0.25X + 0.40Y \leq 40$$

The first two lines are the lower and upper bounds of demand on *X*, the next two are for *Y*, and the last line refers to the productive capacity. Apart from the solution, it is feasible if it satisfies all the constraints. It is optimal if, in addition to being feasible, it yields the best (maximum or minimum) value of the objective function.

As another example, suppose an information center that provides the document delivery service. Standard is one of the documents requested by the customer and provided by the center. The center has an agreement with the BL. BL supplies the documents and gains *$15* per each standard. The center, in contrast, delivers every standard to the user and gains *$20*. The center's profit can be showed through this model:

$$Z = 20X - 15X$$

Where, Z is the profit and X is the total number of standards delivered. The symbols Z and X are *variables*, because no one knows how many standards will be delivered and how much profit will be gained. Z is a *dependent variable*, because its value can be defined upon the number of products sold; and X is an *independent variable*, because no other element affects it in this equation. The numbers *20* and *15* are *parameters*. Parameters are constant values and coefficients of variables. According to the agreement, the center has transferred *$100* to the BL as the prepayment. *$4* is reduced from the center's primary capital per each request. Therefore, another equation is as follows:

$$4X = \$100$$

Now, we have two equations:

$$Z = 20X - 15X$$
$$4X = \$100$$

Consuming *$4* per each standard is called *constraint*. In other words, the center intends to gain more profit (to maximize); while it is limited to the primary capital. The abovementioned equations can be rewritten as follows:

$$\text{Maximize } Z = 20X - 15X$$
Subject to:

$$4X = \$100$$

subject to can also be written as *(s.t)*:

$$\begin{gathered} Maximize\ Z = 20X - 15X \\ s.t: \\ 4X = \$100 \end{gathered}$$

An algebraic operation provides the result:

$$4X = \$100 \Rightarrow X = 100\ /\ \$4 \Rightarrow X = 25\ standards$$

Replace *25* in the first equation as follows:

$$Z = 20X - 15X \Rightarrow Z = \$20\ (25) - \$15\ (25) \Rightarrow Z = \$500 - \$375 = \$125$$

Therefore, if the manager of the information center decided to deliver *25* standards, the center will gain *125* dollars. Subtract the primary capital from the gaining:

$$\$125 - \$100 = \$25$$

The pure profit is *$25*. This means that the center gains one dollar per delivering one document.

4.1.2. Transportation

The transportation model is a special class of absolute models that deals with shipping a commodity from *sources* (e.g., factories) to *destinations* (e.g., warehouses). The objective is to determine the shipping schedule that minimizes the total shipping cost while satisfying supply and demand limits (Rowley and Rowley, 1981; Taha, 2007). While the transportation problem can be modeled as a linear programming model, it is not efficient to solve it in that manner.

In the field of LIS, a vehicle delivers materials to

branches is an example of transportation usage (Reisman and Xu, 1994). Library networks borrowing documents from a number of locations and moving staff between branches in a library system to cover vacancies, holidays, and sick leaves are two other examples (Rowley and Rowley, 1981).

Consider the tableau shown in table 1. This shows unit profit of shipping a common item from four plants to six regional distribution points. Supply refers to the number of units that each destination requires. The "dummy" column is added to the supply-demand matrix so as to make the supply equal the demand. In this table, a dummy demand of 300 units is added to make it equal the total 3600 units of supplies available from four sources. Most transportation problems simply minimize the cost of transportation. This example includes variable production cost, and transportation costs that depend on the distance between the plant and destination.

If the problem were to be modeled as a linear programming model, there would be a decision variable for each combination of shipment. For the example problem, there are 4 sources and 6 possible destinations, resulting in 24 decision variables: the amount shipped from each source to each destination. There would be 10 constraints – 4 indicating the capacity limits on the plants and 6 reflecting the demand constraints. In general, there will be $S \times D$ variables and $S + D$ constraints, where S is the number of sources and D is the number of destinations. For a more realistic problem, there might be a dozen sources and five dozen destinations. Then the linear programming model would have 720 variables and 77 constraints (Lesso, 2007).

A library system that uses central processing is

Table 1 : Transportation problem tableau

	Incremental profit matrix							
Sources	*Destinations*							
	Tehran	*Shiraz*	*Isfahan*	*Tabriz*	*Mashhad*	*Ahvaz*	*Dummy*	*Source supply*
New York	25.00	27.60	40.50	22.50	32.00	48.50	0.00	1200
London	12.00	18.50	30.00	18.00	28.50	32.00	0.00	500
Tokyo	32.60	32.50	48.70	30.80	39.80	52.00	0.00	1200
Paris	21.40	28.00	37.70	22.50	30.50	38.00	0.00	700
Destination demand	750	500	150	750	1000	150	300	3600

another instance. Suppose that library *A* is the responsible body for central processing in a nine-member cooperation system. The problem is to determine the optimum (in this case the least total distance) solution, and hence recommend the route the delivery vehicle should take to go to each branch and return to its starting point. Table 2 represents the distance matrix between the various nodes.

Table 2 : Distance coefficient matrix

	A	*B*	*C*	*D*	*E*	*F*	*G*	*H*	*I*
A	INF	4.8	2.0	1.6	2.8	3.3	4.9	2.3	0.8
B	4.8	INF	3.6	5.6	6.8	1.9	9.6	2.8	5.6
C	2.0	3.6	INF	2.1	4.3	2.0	6.3	2.1	2.8
D	1.6	5.6	2.1	INF	4.0	4.1	4.3	3.5	1.9
E	2.8	6.8	4.3	4.0	INF	6.2	4.3	4.1	2.2
F	3.3	1.9	2.0	4.1	6.2	INF	8.3	2.3	4.5
G	4.9	9.6	6.3	4.3	4.3	8.3	INF	7.1	4.2
H	2.3	2.8	2.1	3.5	4.1	2.3	7.1	INF	2.9
I	0.8	5.6	2.8	1.9	2.2	4.5	4.2	2.9	INF

The first step is to seek a route which starts at *A*. starting at *A*, look for the closest library, i.e., the library with the smallest entry in the matrix in going from *A* to the destination. In our example this is library *I*, so the first delivery in this first route is from *A* to *I*. To move from *I*, ignoring *A* since it has already been visited, choose the destination with the lowest distance coefficient. In this case this is library *D*. applying the same procedure at *D* will lead to library *C* as the next step, and so on. Since destinations are eliminated from consideration once they have been visited, the final route visits all destinations and returns to the origin. It is possible to compute the distance coefficient for this route by adding together all of the individual distance coefficients of each stage.

A similar analysis may be conducted starting at any of the other nodes, yielding a number of alternative routes. These routes are listed in table 3, together with their distance coefficients. It is now an easy matter to compare these routes by examining their distance coefficients. Notice that although neither of these routes starts at *A*, the starting point is arbitrary since the routes are circular and these routes are equally as acceptable as route 1. Close examination of table 3 also reveals that there are three routes stemming from *A*; this situation arises when there is branching. This method of analysis is a simple "rule of thumb" approach to a certain category of problems. The reader is encouraged to check some of the routes shown in table 3 and their corresponding distance coefficients (Rowley and Rowley, 1981).

Table 3 : Routes

1.	*A*	*I*	*D*	*C*	*H*	*E*	*F*	*B*	*G*	*A*	*22.5*
2.	B	F	H	C	A	D	I	E	G	B	40.7
3.	C	A	F	D	H	I	B	E	G	C	25.2
4.	D	A	I	C	H	E	F	G	B	D	27.1
5.	E	I	A	D	I	C	G	F	B	E	34.7
6.	F	B	C	H	A	D	I	E	G	F	32.6
7.	G	I	D	E	A	C	H	F	B	G	49
8.	H	C	A	F	B	I	D	E	G	H	27.1
9.	I	A	D	E	C	H	G	F	B	I	24.9

Another factor in transportation is that the linear programming model matrix will be composed entirely of *0s* and *1s*. Also, these *1s* will be regularly placed. Because of this regular structure, more efficient methods have been found to solve the problem.

These algorithms typically have two phases, just as in linear programming. In the first phase, the objective is to find a feasible solution. One such heuristic is called the North-West Corner rule. Simply stated, the solution process starts in the upper left-hand corner of the tableau, and either the minimum of supply or demand is assigned to the first cell. The next step is to move either horizontally or vertically, depending upon where the demand has been satisfied or the capacity has been all used. The result is a set of assignments that generally move down the main diagonal of the tableau.

A more efficient algorithm is known as Vogel's Approximation Method (VAM). Again using transportation tableau, the procedure is to examine each row and column to determine the difference between the highest unit profit and the next highest unit profit. Where only costs are considered, the procedure would be to determine the difference between the lowest cost and the next lowest cost.

These differences are examined to determine the largest difference, and a transportation assignment is made to the highest unit profit that caused this largest difference. The assignment is to ship either the remaining capacity of the plant or the remaining unsatisfied demand of the destination - whichever is smaller.

The basic philosophy of the VAM is that these differences represent a measure of "regret" – that is, how much would be lost (or how much more would have to be paid) if the row or column representing highest unit profit was not used. That is, if it is not used, then it might be necessary to settle for "second best". Choosing the largest difference is an attempt to minimize regret.

VAM then proceeds to recalculate these differences for the remaining row and columns (one row or column is eliminated at each iteration) and to repeat the procedure. When the method is completed, the result will not only be a feasible solution but an extremely good one – and possibly the optimal. After either approach, the result is an initial basic feasible solution. The next steps are to determine if the solution optimal (Lesso, 2007).

4.1.3. Resource allocation / Assignment

"The best person for the job" is the apt description of the assignment model (Taha, 2007). The assignment problem is an absolute model and a variation of the transportation problem. It can be stated as given a set of N tasks to be performed by N people and a table of values showing the cost or time it takes each person to perform each task, the problem is to minimize the total time or cost it takes to perform the N tasks by choice of which task is assigned to each person, with the restrictions that each task must be done and each person is assigned to only one task.

This can also be considered as a special form of the transportation problem where there are N sources (tasks) and N destinations (people). Also, the capacities are each 1. The linear programming simplifies method to solve the problem can be used. There would be $N \times N$ variables and $2N$ constraints. The matrix also would be all *0s* and *1s*. The transportation algorithm could also be used, but would run into many degenerate solution points.

The special form of the model is used to form a special algorithm to efficiently solve this model. It is known as the Hungarian method and consists of the following steps:

1. The smallest element of the model in each row of the cost-time matrix is subtracted from each element in that row (This will create at least one element that is *0*);

2. The same procedure is repeated for each problem;

3. An attempt is made to make one assignment to each row and column using the elements that are *0* as candidates (The recommended procedure is to start with those rows and columns with only one *0*);

4. If a complete set of assignments has been found; if not, the next step in the procedure is followed;

5. Using a minimum number of lines either horizontal or vertical, the *0s* in each row and column are crossed out (This can always be done, as many lines are assignments in the current solution);

6. The smallest element not crossed out is selected, and it is subtracted from each element not crossed out and added to each element at the intersection of a vertical and horizontal line (This will result in the creation of at least one new *0* as a candidate for assignment and may result in the loss of one or more *0s* if they happened to be at the intersection of two lines); and

7. The entire process is repeated (steps 1-6) until the optimal solution is found.

There are three main categories of allocation problems. The first of these is perhaps the most common type of allocation problem and can be characterized by the following criteria:

1. There is a set of jobs to be done or objectives to be achieved;
2. Enough resources are available for completing all of the jobs;
3. At least one or more of the jobs can be completed in different ways, and thus by using different amounts and types of resources;
4. Some of the ways of doing these jobs are better than others, in that they may be less costly or provide better service; and
5. There are insufficient resources to do each job in the best way.

Another type of allocation problem arises when there are more jobs to be done than available resources permit. Here, the manager must select the jobs which are to be done and decide how resources are to be used in their execution. The last type of allocation problem is when the manger has control over the amount of resources and thus can determine which resources should be added and which are best disposed of or relinquished.

No matter what type of resource allocation there is. The first step in the analysis of any allocation problem is identification of the objective function. The objectives of the system must be decided and expressed in mathematical terms. Typical objectives are to maximize the efficiency of a particular service, maximize profit from an enterprise, or minimize cost.

However, the solution process is reasonably simple and even modestly large problems can be solved by hand. Besides the generic assignment problem, this approach has been used for such diverse applications as the machine change-over problem (the sequence of jobs to be run on a machine to minimize setup time; assigning students to projects; allocating parking spaces to employees; and so forth) (Lesso, 2007).

Assignment or resource allocation is also a common problem in library and information management. The manager has a limited stock of resources, such as money, materials, buildings, and staff to fulfill the library's or information center's objectives in the most effective manner (Kraft and Boyce, 1991). Usually there are constraints on the exploitation of various resources.

Suppose that an information center produces two types of current awareness services and wishes to maximize its profit from its current awareness publications. The center can produce two types of selective dissemination of information service, one based on abstracts and one based on titles, labeled respectively as services *A* and *B*. The center has a potential market of *400* type *A* service and *700* type *B* service. The primary resource used in the production of each service is the staff time involved in scanning, indexing, and abstracting. In addition, there are constraints on the total amount of time that is available for scanning and indexing. More specifically, there is only sufficient scanning time to create *800* copies of either service and there is only adequate indexing time to generate *1000* copies of type *B* service or the equivalent number of type *A* service, with type *A* service requiring twice as much time as type *B* service. Costs incurred in generating the two types of product also relate chiefly to scanning, abstracting, and indexing. Scanning costs, using time spent as a basis, can be estimated at *$1* per service for both type *A* and type *B* services. Abstracting costs are only incurred in producing the abstracting service and are estimated at *$9* per service. Indexing costs are *$4* per copy for the type *A* service, based on abstracts, and *$2* per copy for the type *B* service. The center sells type *A* services for *$18* per profile and type *B* services for *$6* per profile. The center's profit is the difference between revenue from selling the services and costs incurred in producing them. The center wants to know how many services of each type to generate in order to maximize its profit.

Objective function: The objective function is the mathematical expression of those quantities that we wish to optimize. In this instance the unit is concerned to optimize its profit. Profit in this case depends upon the number of services of type *A* and *B* which are generated, so we need some notation to designate these numbers. Then, let:

The number of abstracts-based services (type A) be X1

The number of titles-based services (type B) be X2.

If we wish to investigate the profit further, it is necessary to remember that

Profit = revenue – costs

Now,

The revenue on each service = selling price × number of items sold.

Thus,

Revenue from type A services $= 18X1$
Revenue from type B services $= 6X2$
And so, total revenue $= 18X1 + 6X2$.

Turning our attention to costs, these can be divided as follows:

$$Scanning = X1 + X2$$
$$Abstracting = 9X1$$
$$Indexing = 4X1 - 2X2.$$

The total costs for each operation have been calculated by multiplying the cost per copy for each operation by the number of services of each type.

Then, to account the total cost:

Total cost $= (X1 + X2) + 9X1 + (4X1 + 2X2) = 14X1 + 3X2$.

So, given that

Total profit = total revenue – total cost,

Total profit $= 18X1 + 6X2 - 14X1 - 3X2 = 4X1 + 3X2$.

Thus, the objective function is:

$$Profit = 4X1 + 3X2$$

Constraints: Taking the objective function in isolation, quick inspection will reveal that the most effective means of maximizing profit is to make as many copies of type *A* as possible. But this ready solution must be tempered by other limitations. There is a limit on the number of copies of each type of service that we can expect to sell. These limits can be reflected by the following inequalities:

$$X1 \leq 400$$

$$X2 \leq 700.$$

Other constraints arise from the total time available for the activities necessary to the compilation of a service. These might be stated as:

$$X1 + X2 \leq 800$$

$$2X1 + X2 \leq 1000.$$

Mathematical formulation: To summarize then, the unit's deliberations may be sated as:

$$Maximize\ profit = 4X1 + 3X2$$

$$Such\ that\ X1 \leq 400$$

$$X2 \leq 700$$

$$X1 + X2 \leq 800$$

$$2X1 + X2 \leq 1000$$

Solution: Notice that the objective function

$$Profit = 4X1 + 3X2$$

Involves three variables – profit, *X1*, and *X2* – thus cannot be drawn on a flat piece of paper; the function must, in fact, be represented by a plane. But, *if* we take a specific value of profit, say *200*, *then* the equation becomes:

$$200 = 4X1 + 3X2$$

The values of *X1* and *X2* are:

$$X1 = 200$$

$$X2 = 600$$

Since these values are approximate:

$$X1 + X2 = 800$$

$$2X1 + X2 = 1000$$

By subtraction and substitution we find that

$$X1 = 200 \text{ and } X2 = 600$$

And profit at this point is

$$Profit = (4 \times 200) + (3 \times 600) = 2600.$$

Thus, the information center should compile *200* copies of type *A* current awareness service and *600* copies of type *B* current awareness service, and this will yield a profit of *$2600* (Rowley and Rowley, 1981).

4.1.4. Network

A network consists of a set of *nodes* linked by *arcs* (Kraft and Boyce, 1991). The notation for describing a network is (*N*, *A*), where *N* is the set of nodes and *A* is the set of arcs (Fig. 1).

$$N = \{1, 2, 3, 4, 5\}$$

$$A = \{(1, 2), (1, 3), (2, 3), (2, 5), (3, 4), (3, 5), (4, 2), (4, 5)\}$$

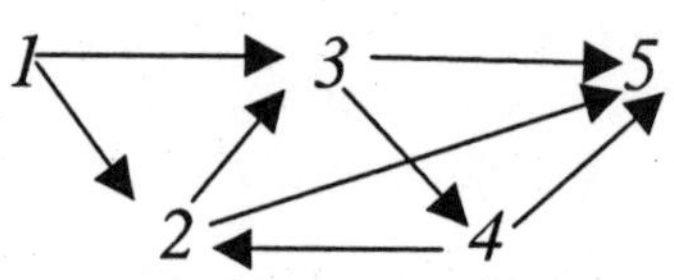

Fig. 1 : A simple network

Associated with each network is a *flow*. In general, the flow in a network is limited by the capacity of its arcs, which may be finite or infinite. An arc is said to be *directed* or *oriented* if it allows positive flow in one direction and zero flow in the opposite direction. A *directed network* has all direct arcs. A *path* is a sequence of distinct arcs that join two nodes through other nodes regardless of the direction of flow in each arc. A path forms a *cycle* or a *loop* if it connects a node to itself through other nodes. For example, in figure one, the arcs (*2, 3*), (*3, 4*), and (*4, 2*) form a cycle. A *connected network* is such that every two distinct nodes are linked by at least one path. The network in figure one demonstrates this type of network.

A *tree* is a *cycle-free* connected network comprised of a subset of all the nodes, and a *spamming tree* is a tree that links all the nodes of the network (Taha, 2007).

In the OR, a multitude of operations research situations can be modeled and solved as networks (nodes connected by branches):

1. Design of computer networks for transferring packages;

2. Determination of the maximum capacity of computer networks in which packages would be transferred;

3. Determination of the shortest route between two or more cities in a regional information service; and

4. Determination of the time schedule (start and completion dates) for the activities of a research project.

In a real example, given the heights and thick-nesses of a given collection of books and the cost of different shelf heights, a network model is developed to determine the optimal number of shelf heights for minimizing shelving costs through finding the shortest path in a directed network (Reisman and Xu, 1994).

Another example has been provided by Rowley and Rowley (1981). Suppose we were engaged in a project to move three crates of books among four libraries, labeled *A*, *B*, *C*, and *D*. The plan of action is that library *A* dispatches one crate to library *D* and two crates to library *B*. subsequently, one of the two crates that library *B* received from *A* is sent to library *C*, and the other is sent to library *D*. The crate sent from library *B* to library *C* is then forwarded to library *D*. We may represent this task in the diagrammatic form shown in Fig. 2.

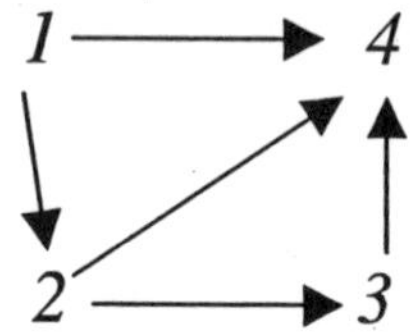

Fig. 2 : Crate migration

In Fig. 2,

Event 1 represents 3 crates leaving A
Event 2 represents 2 crates leaving B
Event 3 represents a crate leaving C
Event 4 represents all 4 crates having arrived at D.

The arrow from *1* to *2* represents the movement of two crates from *A* to *B*, that from *2* to *3* the movement of one crate from *B* to *C*, and so on. Now suppose that the two crates traveling from *A* to *B* are scheduled to take one day in transit, and the crates between *A* and *D*, *B* and *C*, *B* and *D*, and *C* and *D* are scheduled to take *2*, *1*, *3*, and *5* days respectively. Also, assume that one day elapses between the arrival and dispatch of the crates at libraries *B* and *C*. Thus, the time between events *1* and *2* will be $1 + 1 = 2$ days and between events *2* and *3* will be $1 + 1 = 2$ days. We may represent this additional data upon the network in figure 2 with the results shown in figure 3.

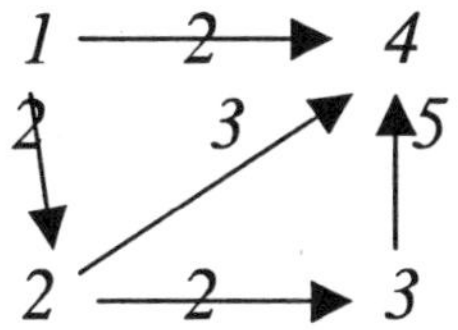

Fig. 3 : Crate migration network with times in transit

Examining Fig. 3, we extract the following information:

Route of the Crates	*Time Taken (in Days)*
1 →4	*2*
1 →2 →4	*2 + 3= 5*
1 →2 →3 →4	*2 + 2 + 5 = 9*

If the crates project is considered completed when all three crates arrive at library *D*, then the total project time will be nine days – the time taken by the route *1 → 2 → 3 → 4*. However, if the time taken by any activity in the sequence *1 → 2 → 3 → 4* were to increase, then the overall time of the project would also increase. But if the time taken by an activity outside the sequence were to increase, for example, say it actually took four days for the crate of books to travel from *A* to *D* (not the scheduled two days), then the overall project time would still be nine days. The sequence *1 → 2 → 3 → 4* is called the critical path of the network shown in figure 3. To reduce the total time of the project, we must attempt to reduce the times of any of the activities *1→ 2*, *2 → 3*, and *3 → 4* (the activities on the critical path). Even if we agree to accept the time of nine days for all the crates to arrive at library *D*, our network can still render us service. From either figure 3 or the table shown above, we note the library *A* could delay the dispatch of the crate to library *D* for up to seven days without increasing the total project time. This fact is usually expressed by the phrase: the activity $1 \rightarrow 4$ has *7* days slack (or has a float of 7 days). In general, the slack of an activity in a project, relevant to a given overall project time, is the amount of time the activity can be expanded by without affecting the overall project time. The table below gives the slack times for each activity of the network in Fig. 3 (with total project time equal to *9* days).

Activity	*Slack*
$1 \rightarrow 2$	*0*
$1 \rightarrow 4$	*7*
$2 \rightarrow 3$	*0*
$2 \rightarrow 4$	*4*
$3 \rightarrow 4$	*0*

Observe that, as would be expected, the activities on the critical path all have zero slack. A list of the slack times for each activity of the project reveals the degree of flexibility and where it is located in the project's strategy as represented by the network. Such a list will assist the project manager in scheduling the project so that it is accomplished in the agreed time while minimizing the overall use of resources.

Minimal spanning tree algorithm: The minimal spanning tree algorithm deals with linking the nodes of a network, directly or indirectly, using shortest total length of connecting branches. A typical application occurs in the construction of paved roads that link several rural towns. The road between two towns may pass through one or more other towns. The most economical design of the road system calls for minimizing the total miles of paved roads, a result that is achieved by implementing the minimal spanning tree algorithm.

The steps of the procedure are given as follows:

Let $N = \{1, 2, \ldots, n\}$ be the best of nodes of the network and define

Ck = Set of nodes that have been permanently connected at iteration k

Ck = Set of nodes as yet to be connected permanently after iteration k

Set $C0 = \varnothing$ and $C0 = N$.

Start with any node i in the unconnected set $C0$ and set $C1 = \{i\}$, which renders

$$C1 = N - \{i\}. \text{ set } k = 2.$$

Select a node, j^*, in the unconnected set $Ck - 1$ that yields the shortest arc to a node in the connected set $Ck - 1$, link j^* permanently to $Ck - 1$ and remove it from $Ck - 1$; that is,

$$Ck = Ck - 1 + \{j^*\}, Ck = Ck - 1 - \{j^*\}$$

In the set of unconnected nodes, Ck, is empty, stop. Otherwise, set $k = k + 1$ and repeat the step.

Shortest-route problem: The shortest-route problem determines the shortest route between a source and destination in a transportation network. Other situations can be represented by the same model.

Shortest-route algorithms: There are two algorithms for solving both cyclic and acyclic networks:

1. Dijkstra's algorithm that is designed to determine the shortest routes between the source node and every other node in the network; and

2. Floyd's algorithm that is general because it allows the determination of the shortest route between any two nodes in the network.

Dijkstra's algorithm: Let *Ui* be the shortest distance from source node *1* to node *i*, and define *dij* (≥ 0) as the length of arc *(I, j)*. Then the algorithm defines the label for an immediately succeeding node *j* as:

$$[Uj,\ i] = [Ui + dij,\ i],\ dij \geq 0$$

The label for the starting node is *[0, _]*, indicating that the node has no predecessor.

Node labels in Dijkstra's algorithm are of two types: *temporary* and *permanent*. A temporary label is modified if a shorter route to a node can be found. If no better route can be found, the status of the temporary label is changed to permanent.

Step 0: Label the source node *(node 1)* with the permanent label *[0, _]*. Set *i* = *1*.

Step i:

(a) Compute the *temporary* labels *[Ui + dij, i]* for each node *j* that can be reached from node *i*, ***provided j is not permanently labeled.*** If node *j* is already labeled with *[Uj, k]* through another node *k* and if *Ui* + *dij* < *Uj*, replace *[Uj, k]* with *[Ui + dij, i]*.

(b) If *all* the nodes have *permanent* labels, stop. Otherwise, select the label *[Ur, s]* having the shortest distance (= *Ur)* among all the temporary labels (break ties arbitrarily). Set $i = r$ and repeat step i.

Floyd's algorithm: Floyd's algorithm is general because it allows the determination of the shortest route between any two nodes in the network (figure 4). The algorithm represents an n-node network as a square matrix with n rows and n columns. Entry (i, j) of the matrix gives the distance dij from node i to node j, which is finite if i is linked directly to j, and infinite otherwise.

The idea of Floyd's algorithm is straightforward. Given three nodes i, j, and k in figure four with the connecting distances shown on the three arcs, it is shorter to reach j from i passing through k if

$$dij + dkj > dik$$

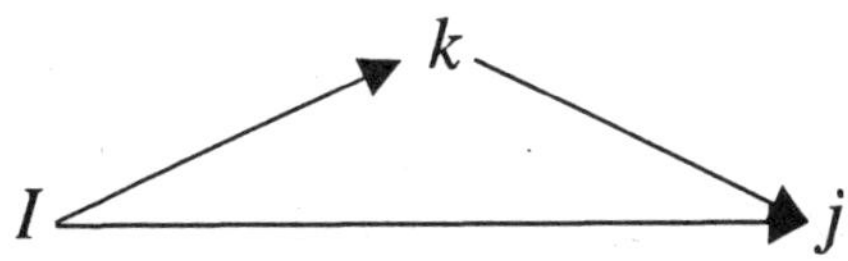

Fig. 4 : Connecting distances of three arcs

In this case, it is optimal to replace the direct route from $i \rightarrow j$ with the indirect route $i \rightarrow k \rightarrow j$. This *triple operation* exchange is applied systematically to the network using the following steps:

Step 0: Define the starting distance matrix $D0$ and node sequence matrix $S0$ as below. The diagonal elements are marked with *(-)* to indicate that they are blocked. Set $k = 1$.

	1	*2*	.	*j*	.	*n*	
	1	-	d12	.	dij	.	d1n
	2	d21	-	.	.	.	.
D0 =	.	.	.	.	.	.	.
	i	di1	di2	.	dij	.	din
	.	.	.	.	.	.	.
	n	*dn1*	*dn2*	.	*dnj*	.	-

		1	*2*	.	*j*	.	*n*
	1	-	2	.	j	.	n
	2	1	-	.	.	.	.
S0 =	.	.	.	.	.	.	.
	i	1	2	.	j	.	n
	.	.	.	.	.	.	.
	n	*1*	*2*	.	*j*	.	-

General step *k*. Define row *k* and column *k* as *pivot row* and *pivot column*. Apply the *triple operation* to each element *dij* in *Dk – 1*, for all *i* and *j*. If the condition

$$dik + dkj < dij, (i \neq k, \text{ and } i \neq j)$$

is stated, making the following changes:

(a) Create *Dk* by replacing *dij* in *Dk – 1* with *dik + dkj*

(b) Create *Sk* by replacing *sij* in *Sk – 1* with *k*. Set *k = k + 1*. If *k = n + 1*, stop; else repeat step *k*.

Step *k* of the algorithm can be explained by representing *Dk – 1*.

Linear programming formulation of the shortest-route problem

The recommended model is general in the sense that it can be used to find the shortest route between two nodes in the network. In this regard, it is equivalent to Floyd's algorithm. Suppose that the shortest-route network includes *n* nodes and that we desire to determine the shortest-route between any two nodes *s* and *t* in the network (Taha, 2007). The linear programming assumes that one unit of flow enters the networks at node *s* and leaves at node *t*.

Define

xij = amount of flow in arc (i, j) = {1, if arc (I, j) is on the shortest route / 0}, otherwise

cij = length of arc (i, j)

Thus, the objective function of the linear program becomes

$$Minimize\ z = \Sigma cijxij$$

The constraints represent the conservation-of-flow equation at each node:

Total input flow = Total output flow

Mathematically, this translates for node *j* to

(External input into node j) + Σxij = (External output from node j) + Σxjk

4.2. PROBABILISTIC MODELS

4.2.1. Basic probability

Probability deals with random outcomes of an *experiment*. The conjunction of all the outcomes is referred to as a *sample space*, and a subset of the sample space is known as an *event* (Taha, 2007). As an illustration, the outcomes of rolling a (six-faced) die are *1, 2, 3, 4, 5, 6*. The set *{1, 2, 3, 4, 5, 6}* defines the associated sample space. An example of an event is that a roll turns up an even value *(2, 4, or 6)*.

An experiment may deal with a continuous sample space as well. For example, the time between failures of an electronic component may assume any nonnegative value.

If an event E occurs m times in an n-trial experiment, then the probability, $P\{E\}$, of realizing the event E is defined as

$$P\{E\} = \lim_{n \to \infty} m / n$$

The definition implies that if the experiment is repeated *indefinitely* $(n \to \infty)$, then the desired probability is represented by m / n. You can verify this definition by flipping a coin and observing its outcome: head *(H)* or tail *(T)*. The longer you repeat the experiment, the closer will be the estimate of $P\{H\}$ or $(P\{T\})$ to the theoretical value of *0.5*.

By definition,

$$0 \leq P\{E\} \leq 1$$

An event E is impossible if $P\{E\} = 0$, and certain if $P\{E\} = 1$. For example, in a six-faced die experiment, rolling a *7* is impossible, whereas rolling an integer value from *1* to *6*, inclusive, is certain.

Addition law of probability

For two events, E and F, $E + F$ $(E \cup F)$ represents the union of E and F, and EF (or $E \cap F$) represents their intersection. The events E and F are mutually exclusive if they do not intersect - that is, if the occurrence of one event precludes the occurrence of the other. Based on these definitions, the addition law of probability can be stated as:

$$P\{E + F\} = \{P\{E\} + P\{F\}, E \text{ and } F \text{ mutually exclusive}, P\{E\} + P\{F\} - P\{EF\}, \text{ otherwise}\}$$

$P\{EF\}$ is the probability that events E and F occur simultaneously.

Conditional law of probability

Given the two events E and F with $P\{F\} > 0$, the conditional probability of E given F, $P\{E \mid F\}$, is defined as:

$$P\{E \mid F\} = P\{EF\} / P\{F\}, P\{F\} > 0$$

If E is a subset of (i.e., contained in) F, then $P\{EF\} = P\{E\}$.

The two events, E and F, are independent if, and only if,

$$P\{E \mid F\} = P\{E\}$$

In this case, the conditional probability law reduces to

$$P\{EF\} = P\{E\} P\{F\}$$

Random variables and probability distributions

The outcomes of an experiment either are naturally numeric or can be coded numerically. For example, the outcomes of rolling a die are naturally numeric – namely, *1, 2, 3, 4, 5, or 6*. Consequently, the testing of an item produces two outcomes: bad and good. In such a case, we use the numeric code *(0, 1)* to represent (bad, good). The numeric representation of the outcomes produces what is known as *random variable*.

A random variable, x, may be *discrete* or *continuous*. For example, the random variable associated with the die-rolling experiment is discrete with $x = 1, 2, 3, 4, 5, or\ 6$, whereas the inter arrival time at a service facility is continuous with $x \geq 0$ (Taha, 2007).

Let's give some examples from the library and information services:

1. Consider a librarian investigating the heights of books. The librarian may decide to subdivide the possible book heights into the ranges: less than or equal to 20 cm., greater than 20 cm. and less than or equal to 25 cm., greater than 25 cm. and less than or equal to 30 cm., and greater than 30 cm. Denote these four ranges, respectively, by *r1, r2, r3, and r4*. Then *{r1, r2, r3, r4}* is a sample space for the experiment of measuring the height of library books since all the possible outcomes are covered once and once only by this set of simple events. Observe that *{r1, r*2, r3, r4}* where *r*2* denotes the range greater than 20 cm. and less than or equal to 28 cm., and where *r1, r3, and r4* are as previously – would not be sample space since the condition of the definition of a sample space is violated.

2. Suppose that a sample of *100* people leaving a library is asked whether they have used a particular facility in the library. The only property of the sample of interest here is the number of people who have used the facility, which will be an integer between *0* and *100*. Thus our sample space should consist of the *101* points *0, 1, 2, . . . , 100*. Every experiment, consisting

of asking a batch of *100* library users about their library usage, is completely described by one of the points in the space. An example, of a compound event would be "a majority of the *100* people sampled used the facility," meaning that the experiment resulted in one of the simple events *51, 52, . . . , 100*.

3. An information officer examining the records of responses to a circulated abstracts bulletin over some time period finds that for each bulletin an average of seven of the thirty people receiving the bulletin make enquiries in response to that bulletin. This situation might be represented by the phrase "the probability of one of the recipients making an enquiry in response to an issue of the bulletin is *7/30*." If in this example, the information officer desires a more detailed picture of the bulletin's usefulness, then the appropriate sample space might be denoted by the set of all sequences of thirty *0s* and *1s*. That is, the sample space would consist of the points *(0, 0, . . . , 0)*, *(1, 0, . . . , 0)*, *(1, 1, 0, 1, 0, . . . , 0)*, etc. The correspondence between a recipient's bulletin use and this sample space is made by assigning to each recipient one of the numbers *1, 2, 3, . . . , 30*. Then the simple event *(1, 0, . . . , 0)* would stand for the event "only recipient number one responded to an issue of the bulletin." And *(0, 1, . . . , 1)* would correspond to the event "an issue of the bulletin resulted in all the recipients numbered *2-30* marking an enquiry, but person number one did not make an enquiry." Here, an example of a composite event would be the subset consisting of all the sequences of thirty *0s* and *1s* which have a *1* in the first place; this is the event "person number one always makes an enquiry."

4. Suppose we wish to discover how effectively a particular database will suit our needs. We prepare, say, *100* typical user profiles. A sample space for the experiment of sending one profile to be processed might consist of the points *(nR, n1)*, the simple event *(nR, n1)* corresponds to the outcome where *nR* relevant and *n1* irrelevant documents are listed from the database. Now we may decide, in order to make some sense of all the numbers we shall be collecting, to "mark" the database's performance on each of the profiles, giving high (low) marks if the ratio *nR / (nR + n1)* is high (low). This ratio is often called precision or precision ratio. This marking, in effect, amounts to giving a mark (number) to each of the simple events in the sample space. For example, we could assign the number *10* to the points *(nR, n1)* with *n1 = 0*, whereas the points *(nR, n1)* with *nR = 0* will be assigned the number *0*. Then the remaining points could be assigned numbers on a sliding scale, depending on the precision they represent.

5. An information unit decides to supply information on request to customers. Data concerning the operation of the information unit is useful for detecting trends in usage, for planning the purchase of information stocks, or for deciding which items may be safely consigned to the storeroom. If this information unit doesn't have its customer operations suitably computerized, then the collection of usage data is likely to be time-consuming. Therefore, the period over which this data can be collected will have to be limited. Consequently, the data obtained will be dominated by the popular information requests and will not represent those pieces of information which didn't happen to be requested during the data

collection period. Suppose the unit wishes to discover user patterns of its information store over a period of a year, but that such data can only be collected for a month. From the data recorded we know the number *nj* of documents that were requested *j* times during the survey month. From this information we want to calculate *mj*, the estimated number of documents that were requested *j* times during the whole year. Of course, we must be careful that the month chosen for the survey is not an atypical one as regards customer demand. We will assume that the *mjs* have been appropriately adjusted for seasonal variations. We make the supposition that the time of request of a particular document is randomly distributed over the year, i.e., the number of request of a document is equally likely to occur in any one of the twelve months of the year. Therefore, of the $m1$ documents requested once in the year, we expect $m1 / 12$ requests to occur in the month when the data is being collected. Thus, we have $n1 = m1 / 12$ and so $12n1 = m1$. Now consider $m2$, the number of documents requested twice during the year. Since $1/12$ is the probability that a particular document is requested in the month, using the following equation $1 - 1/12$ is the probability that it was not requested in that period.

$$P(E) = 1 - P(\text{not } E)$$

Similarly, the probability that another request for the same document did not occur in the sampled period is $1 - 1/12$. We shall also assume that we can neglect the possibility of the document being unavailable to the second customer because the first customer has it. This is equivalent to supposing that the two events are independent. Therefore, using this equation

$$P(F)\,P(E) = P(E\,)\text{''}\,F)$$

the probability that a given document was not requested exactly twice during the survey month is $(1 - 1/12)\,(1 - 1/12) = (1 - 1/12)2$. Consequently, by the first equation in this example, $1 - (1 - 1/12)2$ is the probability of this document being requested exactly twice during the survey period, and so

$$n2 = (1 - (1 - 1/12)2)\,m2.$$
$$m2 = n2\ /\ (1 - (1 - 1/12)2).$$

If we argue along the same lines as above and with the analogous assumption about the independence of the events of document requests, we obtain the general equation

$$mj = nj\ /\ (1 - (1 - 1/12)j),$$

which enables us to derive unbiased estimates from the biased data (Rowley and Rowley, 1981).

4.2.2. Queueing theory

Probably the most studied stochastic process is queueing. A queue or waiting line develops whenever some customer seeks some service that has limited capacity. In other words, its objective is to offer a reasonably satisfactory service to waiting customers (Taha, 2007). Waiting for service is part of our life. This occurs in banks, post offices, doctors' offices, supermarkets, libraries, restaurants, airline check-in counters, and so on. But, it is not limited to human. Queues can also exist in computer centers, repair garages, planes waiting to land at a busy airport, or at a traffic light (Kraft and Boyce, 1991;

Queueing theory, 1994; Rowley and Rowley, 1981).

Queueing theory was first applied to the telephone industry in order to establish acceptable standards for the availability of telephone lines to customers. Subsequent experimentation and theoretical development broadened the scope of application, and operations researchers have used such models to study many different kinds of service situations. Design of shared computer systems to establish standards and priorities in the handling of requests for computer time is another example (Leimkuhler, 1977).

Queueing theory is the prime example of what can be said about the state of the system but not how to improve it. Fortunately, the improvements can be made by increasing the resources available. For example, another teller opens up a window in a bank, or another check-out stand is opened in the supermarket minimizes the frustration of a customer in line behind another with two full shopping carts. Some post offices and banks have gone to a single queue where the person at the head of the line goes to the next available window.

The study of queues deals with quantifying the phenomenon of waiting in lines using representative measures of performance, such as average queue length, average waiting time in queue, and average facility utilization. While it is not possible to generalize the results of queueing analysis, it is possible to provide some general measures. One is the load or traffic factor. This is the ratio of arrival rate to combined service rate, considering the number of service centers in operation. When the load factor *(p)* is low, there is excess serving capacity. There may be occasional lines, but not often. As the load factor rises, a fairly linear rise is obtained in any queueing statistics until approximately the point where $p = 0.75$. After this there is a sharp and continuous rise in the lengths of line and waits. The system is becoming saturated. If $p = 1.00$, the best that can be said is, "the larger the line, the larger the wait".

The following problem is an example of the type of analysis that can be done on a simple queueing system. A check-out counter at a small supermarket can handle customers at a rate of *20* per hour (3 min per customer). Since the number of customers will vary considerably throughout the day and throughout the days of the week, the arrival rate of customers at the check-out counter will also vary considerably. The manager wishes to know when to open up a second check-out counter (Lesso, 2007).

In the library environment, predicting the availability of library materials to the average patron under normal circumstances, evaluating advantages of changing loan periods, acquiring duplicate materials, or restricting items for in-library use have been done using queueing model. W. B. Rose, for example, used queueing to determine the optimal staffing of service desks in libraries and to predict the total volume of circulation of a library collection (Leimkuhler, 1977). The average book circulation time and the mean number of persons who borrow the book will determine the expected circulation rate of that particular book (Reisman and Xu, 1994). In general, document usage is the main research topic in information field susceptible of queuing (Rowley and Rowley, 1981).

Another example of queueing in information field is the delay between the acceptance of a submitted paper to a given journal and its appearance, as introduced by Yu, Li and Yu (2009). The steady state of the publishing process is described as follows: a journal is issued and its various parameters will reach a dynamic equilibrium state after some time, i.e. the state at which no parameters change with time. At steady state, the average publication delay at the *k*th year is:

$$Tk = \tau k + Nk / Yk$$

Where *Tk* is the average publication delay defined as the arithmetic average of publication delay of all papers; τk is the pure publication delay which reflects the editing rapidity of the journal system; and *Nk/Yk* is the ratio of deposited contribution quantity to the publishing capacity which reflects the waiting period of accepted papers deposited in editorial offices. From Equation, we can see that *Tk* is independent of the publishing probability and the distribution strategy that editors select papers to publish by age merely affects the age (or delay) distribution of deposited or published contributions and does not influence publication delays.

Elements of a queueing model

The principle actors in a queueing situation are the *customer* and the *server*. Customers are generated from a source. On arrival at a service facility, they can start service immediately over wait in a queue if the facility is busy. When a facility completes a service, it automatically "pulls" a waiting customer, if any, from the queue. If the queue is empty, the facility becomes idle until a new customer arrives.

From the standpoint of analyzing queues, the arrival of customers is represented by the inter arrival time between successive customers, and the service is described by the service time per customer. Generally, the inter arrival and service times can be probabilistic, as in the operation of a post office, or deterministic, as in the arrival of applicants for job interviews.

Queuing theory analyses queues in terms of four basic features of a system:

1. Arrival pattern;
2. Service pattern;
3. Number of service channels; and
4. Queue discipline.

1. **Arrival pattern:** This pattern describes the rate and distribution of the arrival of members in the queue; it describes the times between the arrivals of units. The arrival pattern may be random or deterministic. It is deterministic if it is possible to predict with reasonable accuracy when the next unit can be expected to arrive as, for instance, in a dentist's waiting room where patients come by appointments. Alternatively, units may arrive at random as exemplified by the breakdown of machinery such as photocopies. The average arrival rate *A* is defined as the number of queue members arriving in a fixed period divided by the length of that period.

2. **Service pattern:** This pattern describes the distribution of times for units to be served. The lengths of services may vary from one customer to the next and among different queuing situations. Service times may all be equal, as with a routine operation such as labeling a book; they may be negligibly small, as with persons passing through an inspection barrier; they may be widely varying, as with the

times taken to answer readers' enquiries; or there may be big gaps in the availability of service, as with batch mode computer searches. The average service rate S is defined as the total number of queue members that can be served in a fixed period divided by the length of that period or as the number of queue units that can be served per minute, hour, or day. It is important to remember that the service rate may not remain constant for any specific queuing situation. Staff may work more efficiently at certain times of the day, or when, for instance, a long queue has formed. Comparing the average arrival rate with the average service rate makes the *traffic intensity* of a queue P.

$$P = A / S$$

If P is larger than *1*, the queuing situation will get out of control since queues of ever increasing length will form. Under such a condition, the average arrival rate A must be bigger than the average service rate S. In other words, on average more units will arrive than can be served in any given unit of time, and thus the queue will continuously grow. In order to avoid infinite queues and to keep the situation under control, the traffic intensity must be less than *1*.

3. **Number of service channels:** This refers to, for example, the number of assistants at the reference desk and the number of PCs for catalog search. Multiple service channels can be in series or parallel. Parallel service channels, such as several assistants at a circulation desk, make service more immediate and reduce queue formation. Systems with service channels in series, i.e., one after the other, are much

more complex to study. As an example of service channels in series, consider a processing department where an information resource is requested, then ordered, acquisitioned, cataloged, classified, labeled, and shelved. This example becomes even more complex when the department follows computerized procedures.

4. **Queue discipline:** The method of determining who shall be served next or given priority is known as queue discipline. People in queues expect fair play, and they expect the First In-First Out (*FIFO*) principle to be in operation. The most common discipline is first come, first served *(FCFS)* or *FIFO*. Other disciplines include last come, first served *(LCFS)* and service in random order *(SIRO)*. But service order need not always mirror arrival order. In the waiting list of hospital treatment, urgent cases are given priority, and in the information services the managing director will be sought first. In fact, customers may be selected from the queue based on some order or priority. The queueing behavior of customers plays a role waiting-line analysis. Human customers may jokey from one queue to another in the hope of reducing waiting time. They may also balk from joining a queue altogether because of anticipated long delay, or they may renege from a queue because they have been waiting too long.

Queue size plays a role in the analysis of queues, and it may have a finite size, as in the buffer area between two successive machines, or it may be infinite, as in mail order facilities. The decision of the service facility may include parallel servers (e.g., post office or bank operation). The servers may also be arranged in series (e.g., job processed by successive machine), or they may be networked (e.g., routers in a computer network). The source from which customers are generated may be finite or infinite. A finite source limits the customers arriving for service (e.g., machines requesting the service of a representation). An infinite source is forever abundant (e.g., calls arriving at a telephone exchange). Variations in the elements of a queueing situation give rise to a variety of queueing models (Kraft and Boyce, 1991; Rowley and Rowley, 1981; Taha, 2007).

Role of exponential distribution

In most queueing situations, the arrival of customers occurs in a totally random fashion. Randomness here means that the occurrence of an event (e.g., arrival of a customer or completion of a service) is not influenced by the length of time that has elapsed since the occurrence of the last event. Random inter arrival and service times are described quantitatively in queueing models by the exponential distribution.

4.2.3. Decision analysis and games

Decision problems involving a finite number of alternative arises frequently in practice. The tools used to solve these problems depend largely on the type of data available (deterministic, probabilistic, or uncertain). The Analytic Hierarchy Process (AHP) is a prominent tool for dealing with decisions under certainty, where subjective judgment is quantified in a logical manner and then used as a basis for reaching a decision. For probabilistic data, decision trees comparing the expected cost (or profit) for the different alternatives are the basis for reaching a decision. Decisions under uncertainty use criteria reflecting the decision maker's attitude toward risk, ranging from optimism to pessimism (Taha, 2007). While not originated by the field of operations research and not strictly in its domain, decision trees are an important tool in the analysis of some stochastic processes. More properly, they are a part of what may be considered statistical decision making (Lesso, 2007). For example, a decision regarding whether or not to install a library security system is addressed given the installation cost and the probabilities of success and failure (Reisman and Xu, 1994). Determining the length of loan period for a given set of materials and for a given set of users, relocating the time and efforts of a transferred staff, and facing with drastic budget cut for the acquisitions department are another instances of the decision analysis (Kraft and Boyce, 1991).

Another tool of decision under uncertainty is game theory, where two opponents with conflicting goals aim to achieve the best out of the worst conditions available to each.

Decision making under risk

Under conditions of risk, the payoffs associated with each decision alternative are described by probability distributions. For this reason, decision making under risk can be based on the *expected value criterion*, in which decision alternatives are compared based on the maximization of expected profit or the minimization of expected cost. However, because the approach has limitations, the expected value criterion can be modified to encompass other situations.

Decision under uncertainty

Decision making under uncertainty, as under risk,

involves alternative actions whose payoffs depend on the (random) states of nature.

Games

Because games are rooted in conflict of interest, the optimal solution selects one or more strategies for each player such that any change in the chosen strategies does not improve the payoff to either player. These solutions can be in the form of a single pure strategy or several strategies mixed according to specific probabilities.

Games with mixed strategies can be solved either graphically or by linear programming. The graphical solution is suitable for games in which at least one player has greatly two pure strategies. The method is interesting because it explains the idea of a saddle point graphically. Linear programming can be used to solve any game problem.

Game theory is particularly appropriate when the outcome of any specified decision is surrounded by an element of uncertainty. Game theory studies the rational components of a decision situation in which uncertainty is present and portrays the situation more explicitly, maximizing the chance of success. The real world involves a complex plethora of technical, behavioral, economic, social, and political considerations. For successful decision making, it is essential to identify the key factors and to simplify the view of the situation.

According to Kraft and Boyce (1991) the elements of any decision-making situation under uncertainty are:

1. A number of possible actions or decisions, only one of which is to be selected;

2. A number of states of nature, or outcomes, dependent on factors outside the control of the decision-maker, any one of which may pertain under any of the decisions taken;

3. The value or consequence to the decision-maker of making any of the possible decisions in light of the possible states of nature; and

4. The criteria or rules by which the decision-maker evaluates and selects alternatives.

A game is such a decision-making situation. It is a contest between players, which is played for fun or forfeit, according to some predetermined rules. The game's outcome is decided by skill, strength, or chance.

Rowley and Rowley (1981) have provided an illustration of the game theory utilization in information services. They considered a situation in which a library manager has to choose among four different maintenance arrangements for computer equipment. Three maintenance firms offer three distinct contracts, and the fourth firm is prepared to come out on demand without a prior contract. The substance of the four contracts available is:

Contract	*Breakdown calls*	*Annual cost for contract*	*Cost for each extra call*
1	*1 call free*	*5*	*6*
2	*2 calls free*	*10*	*6*
3	*3 calls free*	*12*	*6*
None	*0 calls free*	*0*	*7*

In other words, contract 1 specifies that the maintenance engineer will attend 1 breakdown call free as part of the total service which will cost 5 units per year. Any calls in excess of one per year will be charged at 6 units. Likewise, the second and third contracts have annual charges and charge extra for any calls in excess of the specified number. The forth possibility is to spurn a contract and pay 7 units for each on demand call.

Now, if it is assumed that there can be a maximum of four breakdowns in any given year, then the payoff matrix facing the decision-maker can be shown as:

	0	*1*	*2*	*3*	*4*
Contract 1	*–5*	*–5*	*–11*	*–17*	*–23*
Contract 2	*–10*	*–10*	*–10*	*–16*	*–22*
Contract 3	*–12*	*–12*	*–12*	*–12*	*–18*
Contract 4	*0*	*–7*	*–14*	*–21*	*–28*

4.3. MIXED MODELS

4.3.1. Dynamic programming

Dynamic programming (DP) determines the optimum solution of a multivariate problem by decomposing it into stages, each stage comprising a single variable sub-problem. The advantage of the decomposition is that the optimization process at each stage involves one variable only. A DP model is basically a recursive equation linking the different stages of the problem in a manner that guarantees that each stage's optimal feasible solution is also optimal and feasible for the entire problem (Taha, 2007).

This technique is not as structured as linear programming, and more properly should be referred to as a solution philosophy rather than a solution technique. Actually, predecessors of this philosophy have been known for some time under the general classification of calculus of variations methods. Dynamic programming is based on the principle of optimality as expressed by Richard Bellman: "An optimal policy has the property that whatever the initial state and initial decision are, the remaining decision must constitute an optimal policy with regard to the state resulting from the first decision". The operative result of this principle is to start at the "end" of the problem – the last stage of the decision making process – and "chain back" to the beginning of the problem, making decisions at each stage that are optimal from that point to the end (Lesso, 2007).

However, there are famous models designed on the DP idea including:

Knapsack/Fly-Away/Cargo-Loading Model

The knapsack model classically deals with the situation in which a soldier must decide on the most valuable items to carry in a backpack. The problem paraphrases e general resource allocation model in which a single limited resource is assigned to a number of alternatives with the objective of maximizing the total return (Taha, 2007).

The backward recursive equation is developed for the general problem of an n-item *W-1b* knapsack. Let *mi* be number of units of item i. The general problem is represented by the following ILP:

$$Maximize\ z = r1m1 + r2m2 + \ldots + rnmn$$

Subject to

$$w1m1 + w2m2 + \ldots + wnmn \leq W$$
$$m1, m2, \ldots, mn \geq 0 \ and\ integer$$

The three elements of the model are

1. *Stage i* is represented by item i, $i = 1, 2, \ldots, n$.

2. The *alternatives* at stage i are represented by mi, the number of units of item i included in the knapsack. The associated return is $rimi$. Defining $[W / wi]$ as the largest integer less than or equal to W / wi, it allows that $mi = 0, 1, \ldots, [W / wi]$.

3. The *state* at stage i is represented by xi, the total weight assigned to stages (items) i, $i + 1$, ..., and n. This definition reflects the fact that the weight constraint is the only restriction that links all n stages together.

Define

$fi(Xi)$ = maximum return for stages i, $i + 1$, and n, given state xi

The simplest way to determine a recursive equation is a two-step procedure:

Step 1. Express $fi(Xi)$ as a function of $fi(xi + 1)$ as follows:

$$fi(Xi) = min\ \{rimi + fi + 1\ (xi + 1)\},\ I = 1, 2, \ldots, n$$
$$fn + 1\ (Xn + 1) = 0\,.$$

Step 2. Express $Xi + 1$ as a function of Xi to ensure that the left-hand side, $fi(Xi)$, is a function of Xi only. By definition, $Xi - Xi + 1 = wimi$, represents the weight used at stage i. Thus, $Xi + 1 = Xi - wimi$, and the proper recursive equation is given as

$$fi(Xi) = max \{rimi + fi + 1\ (Xi - wimi)\},\ I = 1, 2, \ldots, n$$

Work-Force Size Model

In some construction projects, hiring and firing are exercised to maintain a labor force that meets the needs of the project. Given that the activities of hiring and firing both incur additional costs, how should the labor force be maintained throughout the life of the project (Taha, 2007)?

Let us assume the project will be executed over the span of n weeks and that the minimum labor force required in week i is bi laborers. Theoretically, we can use hiring and firing to keep the work-force in week i exactly equal to bi. Alternatively, it may be more economical to maintain a labor force larger than the minimum requirements through new hiring.

Given that xi is the actual number of laborers employed in week i, two costs can be incurred in week i: $C1\ (xi - bi)$, the cost of maintaining an excess labor force $xi - bi$, and $C2\ (xi - xi - 1)$, the cost of hiring additional laborers, $xi - xi - 1$. It is assumed that no additional cost is incurred when employment is discounted.

The elements of the DP model are defined as follows:

1. *Stage* i is represented by week i, $i = 1, 2, \ldots, n$.
2. The *alternatives* at stage i are xi, the number of laborers in week i.
3. The *state* at stage i is represented by the number of laborers available at stage (week) $i - 1$, $xi - 1$.

The DP recursive equation is given as

$$fi(xi - 1) = \min \{C1(xi - bi) + C2(xi - xi - 1) + fi + 1(xi)\},\ I = 1, 2, \ldots, n$$

The computations start as stage n with $xn = bn$ and terminate at stage 1.

Equipment Replacement Model

The longer a machine stays in service, the higher is its maintenance cost, and the lower its productivity. When a machine reaches a certain age, it may be more economical to replace it. The problem thus reduces to determining the most economical age of a machine (Taha, 2007).

Suppose that we are studying the machine replacement problem over a span of n years. At the start of each year, we decide whether to keep the machine in service an extra year or to replace it with a new one. Let $r(t)$, $c(t)$, and $s(t)$ represent the yearly revenue, operating cost, and salvage value of a t-year-old machine. The cost of acquiring a new machine in any year is i.

The elements of the DP model are:

1. *Stage* i is represented by year i, $i = 1, 2, \ldots, n$.
2. The *alternatives* at stage (year) i call for either *keeping* or *replacing* the machine at the *start* of year i.
3. The *state* at stage i is the age of the machine at the start of year i.

Given that the machine is t years old at the *start* of year i, define

$fi(t)$ = *maximum net income for years* i, $i + 1, \ldots,$ *and* n

The recursive equation is derived as

$$fi(t) = max \{r(t) - c(t) + fi + 1\ (t + 1),\ if\ KEEP$$

Or

$$r(0) + s(t) + I - c(0) + fi + 1(1),\ if\ REPLACE\}\ fn + 1(.) \equiv 0$$

4.3.2. Simulation

Simulation is defined as the essence of reality without reality itself. According to Taha, it is the next best thing to observing a real system (2007) or the act of experimenting with a model and observing the consequences (Rowley and Rowley, 1981). With stochastic processes, values are simulated for the random variables from their known or assumed probability distribution, a simpler model is solved, and the process is repeated a sufficient number of times to obtain statistical confidence in the results. In other words, simulation models are more concerned with describing how very complicated systems behave and predicting the future state of such systems as a result of chance events and deliberate changes in their configurations (Leimkuhler, 1977).

Basically, simulation views an operational situation as a waiting line in a service facility. By literally following the movements of customers in the facility, pertinent statistics (e.g., waiting time and queue length) can be collected. The task of using simulation starts with the development of the logic of the computer model in a manner that will allow collecting needed data (Taha, 2007).

As a simple example of this, assume that someone makes the statement that the average female student at a university is of a certain height. To verify this assumption the actual heights of female students could be measured, but this may be a long process. As an alternative, a hopefully random sample may be taken, the heights measured, the average determined, and an inference made as to the whole female population.

Many stochastic processes do not lend themselves to such a direct approach. Instead of assumption is made as to what the underlying probability distributions of the random variables are, and these are sampled. This sampling is done with random numbers. True random numbers are difficult to obtain, so pseudorandom numbers are generated by some mathematical relationship. This apparent paradox is justified by the fact that the numbers appear to be random and pass most tests for randomness. As an example, a queueing system could be modeled by having two wheels of fortune – one with numbers in random order from 1 to 15, and the other from 1 to 20. The first could represent the number of arrivals into the system per 10-min period, and the other the number served during the same period. In this manner a system with a load factor of 0.75 could be simulated. Many simulation computer languages have been developed to ease the work of analyzing queueing systems (Lesso, 2007).

Elements of discrete-event simulation

1. **Generic definition of events:** All discrete-event simulations describe, directly or indirectly, queueing situations in which customers arrive, wait in queue if necessary, and then receive service before they depart the system. In general, any discrete-event model is composed of a network of interrelated queues. Given that a discrete-event model is in reality a composite of queues, collection of simulation statistics (e.g., queue length and status of the service

facility) take place only when a customer arrives or leaves the facility. This means that two principle events control the simulation model: arrivals and departures. These are the only two instants at which we need to examine the system. At all other instants, no changes affecting the statistics of the system take place.

2. **Sampling from probability distribution:** Randomness in simulation arises when the interval, *t*, between successive events is probabilistic. There are three methods for generating successive random samples $(t = t1, t2, \ldots)$ from a probability distribution $f(t)$:

   a. *Inverse method* : Obtaining a random sample x from the probability density function $f(x)$.

   b. *Convolution method* : Expressing the desired sample as the statistical sum of other easy-to-sample random variables.

   c. *Acceptance-rejection method* : Replacing the complex $f(x)$ with a more analytically manageable proxy $h(x)$.

However, there are many instances of using simulation in information field. For example, with the number of staff, the volumes of various jobs (e.g., users' requests, new issues, overdue fees) and the job processing times specified, simulation is used to estimate the delays, processing times, and utilization of each member of the staff and the whole facility of a given library (Reisman and Xu, 1994). Interior design (Cook, 1968), book reservation service (Baumler and Baumler, 1975), queuing at a reference desk (Regazzi and Hersberger, 1976), and loan and duplication policies (Buckland and et al, 1970) have also been investigated using simulation. For about three decades, simulation models were designed using computer programs. Several programs have yet been developed for loan policies and book availability (Shaw, 1975), document delivery (Probst Reed, 1976), and provision of library services (Thomas and Robertson, 1975).

One of the latest studies done by Yu, Li and Yu (2009) is related to the publishing cycle of scientific papers. They have illustrated that the process of publishing or scholarly communication could be modeled through mathematical formulae. According to them, there are three stages in the scientific production process including:

1. Identifying, locating, assessing, analyzing, developing, expressing new ideas, submission of manuscripts, called contributions for potential publication;
2. Peer review, revision, acceptance of eligible manuscripts and rejection of below standard manuscripts; and
3. Editing time and waiting time for publication of accepted contributions, called eligible products.

In their inference, the quantity of accepted contributions per unit time is defined as actual output *X* of scientific products. The quantity of published contributions per unit time is defined as quantity *Y* of published papers, namely, the statistic of the scientific output indicator. The quantity of contributions deposited in the water tank, called inventory of scientific products, is expressed by *N*. It is obvious that a change in *Y* reflects a change in *X* to a certain extent and *N* would increase if *Y* were more than *X*.

For a certain journal, supposing No. k issue, the variables describing the process are defined as follows:

- Xk represents the quantity of papers accepted in the interval between No. k and No. $k + 1$ issue, namely, the accepted contribution flux or the actual scientific output in the interval;
- τk is the actual publication delay, which is the reviewing time (about 1–3 months or so);
- Ti is the age of the deposited contribution from the received date of a manuscript in i node;
- Nk expresses the inventory of papers before No. k issue is published, also called backlog of accepted contributions;
- nk (Ti) represents the deposited paper age distribution before No. k issue is published;
- Pk (Ti) is the age distribution function of the deposited contribution publishing probability of No. k issue;
- Yk is the quantity of published papers in No. k issue, namely, the capacity or the scientific output statistic of the journal (or journal group) in the interval; and
- yk (Ti) is the age distribution of the published papers in No. k issue.

The relation between these variables is described by equation:

$$Nk + 1 = Nk + (Xk - Yk)\,.\Delta t$$
$$Nk = \Sigma \infty i = 0\; nk\; (Ti).\Delta T$$
$$Yk = \Sigma \infty i = 0\; yk\; (Ti).\Delta T\; (1)$$

$$nk + 1(Ti{+}1) = nk\ (Ti)\ yk\ (Ti).\Delta T$$
$$yk\ (Ti) = Pk\ (Ti).\ nk\ (Ti)$$
$$nk\ (\tau) = Xk\ /\ \Delta T$$

where $Nk{+}1 = Nk + (Xk - Yk)$ expresses the difference equation of the inventory of contributions; $Nk = \Sigma\infty\ i = 0$ $nk(Ti).\Delta T\ \Delta T$ expresses the relationship of the inventory (the deposited contribution quantity) and its age distribution; $Yk = \Sigma\infty i = 0\ yk(Ti).\Delta T$ expresses the relationship of the published contribution quantity and its age distribution; $nk{+}1(Ti{+}1) = nk(Ti)\ yk(Ti).\ \Delta T$ expresses the difference equation of the deposited manuscript age distribution and the published contribution age distribution; $yk(Ti) = Pk(Ti).nk(Ti)$ expresses the age distribution function of the publishing probability of deposited contribution; and $nk(\tau) = Xk / \Delta T$ expresses the boundary condition of equation.

In equation, the initial condition is: $T0 = \tau$, $Nk{=}0 = N0$, $Xk{=}0 = X0$, and $Yk = 0 = Y0$. Considering the intrinsic dispersion characteristic, let k represent the number of issues of a periodical; let i represent the differential node point of the literature age, namely, the delay value when the literature is published; let ΔT represent the interval between two differential node points of the literature age; let ΔT represent the interval between continuous two issues; and, for convenience of computing, let ΔT and Δt be defined as one month (or year).

It is the prerequisite of setting the initial values for the simulation of the adjusting process that all deposited contributions have an average published probability at steady state. The characteristic of a steady state is that the parameters are not changed with time, namely, No. k issue in the discrete model. In equation, the quantity of accepted manuscripts is equal to the quantity of published contribution flux when $k = 0$, namely, $X0 = Y0$. We can give $N0$ different values and simulate the adjusting process. According to the particular solution of the model and the equation of publishing probability at steady state (the most simple age distribution of the literature publishing probability: $P0\ (Ti) = P0 = const.$), we obtain the initial condition of the process simulation thus:

$$P0 = Y0 \,/\, N0$$
$$y0 = P0\,(1-P0)\; i\,.X0 / \Delta T$$
$$n0 = (1-P0)\; i\,.X0 / \Delta T$$

Above equations are recurrence formulae of the parameters from one steady state to another and can be used to simulate the change process of the deposit inventory along with changes in parameters X and Y.

5 OR in the LIS field

5.1 OVERVIEW

Philip Morse and his followers have studied libraries as environments capable of using operations research methods. Morse was a colleague of Vannevar Bush at the Massachusetts Institute of Technology (MIT) and first president of the Operations Research Society of America. He studied library problems partly because of his genuine interest and concern in this area, and partly because the university library was a convenient and rich laboratory for his students at MIT. Similar reasons along with financial support from the National Science Foundation's Office of Science Information Service, prompted several other university-based operations research groups to give special attention to library problems. The participants in these studies and their work have spread to other institutions and have merged with the efforts of two other groups, those concerned primarily with the development of new kinds of information systems and those concerned primarily with the development of the field of information science. The former group was more in line with the ideas of Vannevar Bush and was computer oriented. The latter group was more directly in the tradition of library science and was concerned with the mathematical and logical description of basic phenomena in information processes.

The practical motivation on the part of library mangers for operations research studies was the pressure to economize and expand activities by means of computers.

Operations research was seen as the best way to conduct exploratory studies before making costly commitments for new computerized systems. The need was for logical models of the library that can be experimented with in order to see what was most useful and what data were needed to make a new synthesis of libraries and computers work most effectively. One needed to anticipate the management problems of new systems in order to design the appropriate feedback and control devices. The initial task was to model the library as it functioned and then to experiment with new systems. The preoccupation with existing systems was necessary to form a sound basis for predicting the effects and guiding the development of innovations (Leimkuhler, 1977).

The literature reveals a holistic view of OR in libraries within the following categories:

- Provision of building area
  - Centralization versus decentralization
  - Branch location
- Hours
- Seating and space utilization
- Selection of documents
  - Choice of book subject matter and year
  - Number of copies
  - Theoretical foundation of journal selection
  - Journal selection
  - Selection effort

   — Acquisition of document

- Processing of documents
   — Processing work flow
   — Binding of serials
- Classification and cataloging of documents
   — Indexing
   — Original versus temporary cataloging
   — DDC and LCC correlation
   — Cataloging at the Library of Congress
   — Catalog use
- Control of location and use of documents
   — Selection of materials for compact storage
   — Storage of library materials
   — Load period
   — In-library use
- Security guards
   — Return of circulated library materials
- Facilitation of use of documents
   — Photo duplication
- Maintenance and weeding of documents
   — Book relabeling
   — Book weeding

- — Journal weeding
- Aids for location of documents in other libraries
- Facilitation of access to other libraries
  - — Interlibrary borrowing decision rules
  - — Retrieval systems
  - — Networks
  - — Personal assistance
- Publications, advertisements and exhibits
  - — Library initiative communication
  - — Planning and administration
  - — Library legislation
  - — Library/user/funder analysis
  - — Participative decision making
  - — Data processing
  - — Projecting library growth
  - — Overall university library resource allocation
  - — Overall public library resource allocation (Reisman and Xu, 1994).

Also, Rowley and Rowley (1981) list major areas for the application of OR as follows:

I. Practical problems amendable to OR

A. Recurrent problems

1. Resource allocation
2. Long-term planning
3. Advertising library services
4. Marketing information services

B. On-off decisions

1. Library location
2. Investment in new facilities

C. Control systems design

1. Policies for acquisition of stock (including duplication)
2. Loan policy
3. Decision rules for inter-borrowing
4. Weeding policy
5. Staff levels and career planning

D. Other design problems

1. Information service design
2. Management information systems for libraries

II. Themes for enabling research

A. Toward developing management skills

1. Management gaming
2. Developing diagnostic tools

B. Toward improving the effectiveness of management research

1. Questionnaire design

2. Developing other measuring instruments

3. Data banks

C. Toward A and B

1. Developing measures of effectiveness

2. The meta-system (especially user behaviour)

While there are overlaps in these two holistic views, there is a clear distinction between the library-oriented view point of Reisman and Xu (1994) and the management-oriented view point of Rowley and Rowley (1981). As a whole, literature on the utilization of OR in libraries has classified the field in several different ways. Reisman and Xu (1994) classify the literature in the detailed fashion outlined above. Kantor (1979) classifies papers and projects into five groups according to the purpose of the research: *system description*; *modeling the system*; *parameter identification*; *optimization or multi-valuation*; and *application*; while Rowley and Rowley (1981) classify the work by the nature of the research (e.g., *recurrent problems*, *on / off decisions*). Nevertheless, they can be categorized in another form, as follows:

5.2 USAGE STUDIES

Operations research models that have been developed within library settings tend to focus on the library as a document storage and retrieval center. Traditionally, the majority of information in a library stored appeared in monograph and periodical forms; i.e. books and journals. Usage, in general, can be predicted over time to follow a mathematical model. Such a model is used to detect some interesting differences in the usage patterns of information in different subject fields. The model is then used to make policy recommendations for such activities as acquisition, organization, circulation, retirement, storage and retrieval (Leimkuhler, 1977). Usage studies are still conducted based on log file analysis.

5.3 LIBRARY STORAGE PROBLEMS

Many library usage studies were motivated by the search for more efficient methods of storing library materials that would minimize the inconvenience to users by discarding little-used materials or storing them in less accessible locations. The use of a depository for little-used materials was the subject of some major studies. In these studies, several low cost decision rules for the selection of library materials for compact storage were developed. Generally, two types of rules developed from these studies:

1. Using time since publication or acquisition as the determining factor; and

2. Using some measure of current activity as the selection criteria.

In a clearer word, when a simple exponential growth model is combined with the exponential obsolescence model, then the total circulation of the collection will increase proportionally to the size of the collection, depending on the growth and obsolescence rates. In this way, it is possible to predict how much circulation demand will be generated by a depository collection where age is the determining factor. This model can also be used to show

how the average cost of circulation might be minimized by use of a depository. Apart from the location of the depository, the physical attributes of the collection storage is another factor affecting information services. Suppose a collection with many items of unusual small and large dimensions. By describing the dimensional characteristics of a collection in a mathematical manner, the resulted model shows how to determine the gain in storage capacity by using size as a criterion by shelving. Mathematical techniques and statistical methods have yet been perfected for explaining the physical attributes of the collection. In general, such studies are able to demonstrate the extent to which improvement in shelving capacity might be gained by using such methods, which is rather limited for most collections but could be very important in large depositories. In addition to their reinforcement of the need for better cost data and other statistical information about libraries, these models also opened the way for demonstrating the applicability of the optimization techniques used in operations research. They also serve to bring into sharper focus the real material-handling problems in document systems. Models of this kind are also applicable to other kinds of information storage systems using computers and miniaturization, and possible to the eventual procedure of transferring information from one kind of system to the other. For example, graph theory can be used to model networks of storage and retrieval centers (Leimkuhler, 1977).

5.4 AVAILABILITY, LOAN AND DUPLICATION POLICIES

Providing better access to the information is an ideal point for information systems. Better access means that the document is more likely to be available at the time and place it is sought either as a specific request or as part of a larger search for information. The decision problems in regard to the better access include:

1. The amount and allocation of resources budgets;
2. The purchase of duplicate copies;
3. The placement of information resources in open shelves, stacks, and reserve collections;
4. Changes in loan policies;
5. Control of losses; and
6. Limitations on shelf space and the use of storage areas.

The approach taken is to estimate how many users will be inconvenienced as a result of changes in retirement, duplication, circulation, reshelving, and replacement of lost resources, and then to compare these various measures of effectiveness with the Dollar/Euro cost of making improvements. In these studies, the effect of satisfaction level, that is, the probability of a book for example on a shelf when requested is calculated for various combinations of loan period, number of copies, amount of in-library use, and the probability that a user will ask that an information resource be recalled or reserved. These calculations are made by means of a computer simulation model and show the overall satisfaction level. The new model may lead to a surprisingly large increase in the number of items borrowed (Leimkuhler, 1977; Linn, 2007). Warwick and Bell paraphrases the same statement on determining correct loan and duplication policies and predicting the changes in demand for sections of the book stock (2009). For example, if loan periods are shortened as a substitute for buying extra copies (book circulation would be increased) it may be the case that library users become dissatisfied with the service and seek alternatives thus reducing demand for the texts. Conversely, buying extra copies may initially improve the service and might encourage greater use of the library thus increasing demand and negating the effect of providing extra titles. These types of changes require careful monitoring of system change after policy or operational changes.

5.5. REFERENCE SERVICES AND DOCUMENT ACQUISITION MODELS

Attempts to formulate rules for the selective acquisition of library materials through the use of mathematical models have usually been associated with journals collections and the seminal work of S. C. Bradford. Bradford's Law can be used to estimate the total number of papers that will be found if a complete search is made of the literature, as well as the total number of journals that will contain at least one relevant article. By partially ordering or classifying a file of journals according to their productivity, the expected time it takes to search for a particular piece of information can also be greatly reduced. In particular, the benefits from a two or three stage search procedures are relatively very large when compared to the advantages of more exhaustive classification schemes. The journal selection problem can be formulated as a multiple choice model in which one seeks to determine the optimal allocation of present and future (expected) funds for purchasing journals, using a criterion based on expected usage as a measure of journal value. A book selection model for a public library which attempts to maximize the benefit the library provides to the community for a given book budget was developed. Benefit is measured by estimating the circulation of a book and the present Dollar/Euro value of the circulations. The Dollar/Euro value is based on the price of the book, the proportion of borrowers who would otherwise buy the book, and the benefit of borrowing expressed as a fraction of the purchase price. The product of these factors is discounted over the life of the book in order to determine the equivalent lifetime benefit of a book in terms of present Dollars/Euros. By combining this measure with the cost of acquisition to form a benefit/cost ratio, the library can determine a rank ordering of the relative advantage of purchasing different classes of books (Leimkuhler, 1977).

5.6. DIFFICULTIES OF OR APPLICATION

Science production, strategic planning, document delivery, holding control, transportation, management, research, quality control, repair and maintenance, locating, and repackaging are susceptible areas of LIS for OR. However, it must be kept in mind that the application of operations research models in the planning and control of an organization requires a considerable effort in collecting experimental data and testing the model for its applicability to a given situation. Furthermore, the actual use of such models on a day-to-day basis requires the input of reliable data on a regular basis. For this reason, operations research work often leads to substantial revisions in the way information is processed in an organization.

Despite the numerous theoretical studies reported in the literature, there is very little evidence of such studies being used to make any major changes in operational library systems. The slowness with which fundamental changes in library methods have emerged over the last several decades is due to several factors including:

- Too much attention has been devoted to the construction, and solution of complex mathematical models (Kraft and Boyce, 1991; Rowley and Rowley, 1981);
- Too little attention has been placed on the implementation aspect of an operations research model;
- Too little emphasis has been focused upon the process of operations research;
- Too little attention has been placed on the pressing strategic problems of library managers (Bommer, 1975);
- The library has a past which affects its future, i.e. traditions and organizational culture determines many visible and invisible factors controlling the quantity and quality of the library services;
- Antipathy on the part of librarians in making use of operations research techniques;
- Financial limitations of libraries to support research activities of this kind;
- Ignoring the operations research methods and techniques in LIS education, partly because of unfamiliarity of tutors and partly because of technological trends governing the LIS schools;
- The scope and complexity of the task of making fundamental changes in library methods, because of

impossibility of isolating any single library from the regional, national and even international environment in which it operates;

- The human element that is an important factor in the design of libraries and information systems (Leimkuhler, 1977).

As reflected in the literature, there is a gap between the complex mathematical models in OR and not well-educated library workers. OR analysts could also be criticized for not idealizing the existing library systems, not gathering data, and not building models on faulty bases. To enhance the application of OR in libraries, a closer working relationship between operations researchers and library managers is suggested.

References

6.1 CITED WORKS

1. "Linear programming". (1994). In: Parker, S. P. (Ed.), *McGraw-Hill Concise Encyclopedia of Science and Technology*. New York: McGraw-Hill, 990-991.

2. "Operations research". (1994). In: Parker, S. P. (Ed.), *McGraw-Hill Concise Encyclopedia of Science and Technology*. New York: McGraw-Hill, 1201.

3. "Queueing theory". (1994). In: Parker, S. P. (Ed.), *McGraw-Hill Concise Encyclopedia of Science and Technology*. New York: McGraw-Hill, 1437.

4. Baumler, J. V. and Baumler, J. L. (1975). A simulation of Reserve Book Activities in a College Library Using GPSS/360. *College and Research Libraries*, Vol. 36, No. 3: 222-227.

5. Bommer, M. (1975). Operations Research in Libraries: A Critical Assessment. *Journal of the American Society for Information Science*, Vol. 26, No. 3: 137-139.

6. Buckland, A., et al. (1970). *Systems Analysis of a University Library*. Lancaster: Publisher name and contact information, as provided by the publisher; updated only if notified by the publisher.The Librarian, University of Lancaster Library.

7. Calderhead, V. (1997). An Operations Research

Approach to a Chemistry Library Relocation: Measure Often, Move Once. *Science & Technology Libraries*, Vol. 16, No. 1: 61–80.

8. Churchman, C. W. (1972). Operations Research Prospects for Libraries: The Realities and Ideals. *The Library Quarterly*, Vol. 42, No. 1: 6-14.
9. Cook, J. J. (1968). Increased Seating in the Undergraduate Library: A Study in Effectiveness Space Utilization. In Burkhalter, B. R. (Ed.), *Case Studies in Systems Analysis in a University Library*. Metuchen, N.J.: Scarecrow Press, 142-170.
10. Kantor, P. (1979). Review of Library Operations Research. *Library Resources*, Vol. 1, No. 4: 295-345.
11. Kraft, D. H. and Boyce, B. R. (1991). *Operations Research for Libraries and Information Agencies: Techniques for the Evaluation of Management Decision Alternatives*. San Diego: Academic Press.
12. Leimkuhler, F. F. (1972). Library Operations Research: A Process of Discovery and Justification. *The Library Quarterly*, Vol. 42, No. 1: 84–96.
13. Leimkuhler, F. F. (1977). Operations Research. In: A. Kent et al (Eds.), *Encyclopedia of Library and Information Science*. New York: Marcel Dekker. Inc. Vol. 20: 412-439.
14. Lesso, W. G. (2007). Operations Research. In: J. Weil et al (Eds.), *McGraw-Hill encyclopedia of science and technology*. New York: McGraw-Hill. Vol. 12: 390-397.
15. Linn, M. (2007). Budget systems used in allocating resources to libraries. *Bottom Line: Managing*

Library Finances, Vol. 20, No. 1: 20-29.

16. Ma, T -J. (1997). Operations research in library science. *Journal of Educational Media & Library Sciences*, Vol. 34, No. 4: 405-421.

17. Nkereuwem, E. E. and Eteng, U. (1994). The Application of Operations Research in Library Management: A Case Study of In-library Book Use. *Library Review*, Vol. 43, No. 6: 37-43.

18. Reed, M. J. P. (1976). Computer Simulation: A Tool for Analysis of Library Services. *Journal of Library Automation*, Vol. 9, No. 2: 117-136.

19. Regazzi, J. J. and Hersberger, R. (1976). Queues and Reference Service Inference: A Simulation of a Library Reference Desk. In Martin, S. K. (Ed.), *Information Politics: Proceedings of the 39th ASIS Annual Meeting*. San Francisco: American Society for Information Science.

20. Reisman, A. and Xu, X. (1994). Operations Research in Libraries: A Review of 25 Years of Activity. *Operations Research*, Vol. 42, No. 1: 34-40.

21. Rowley, J. E. and Rowley, P. J. (1981). *Operations research: A tool for library management*. Chicago: American Library Association.

22. Shaw, W. M. (1975). Computer Simulation of the Circulation Subsystem of a Library. *Journal of the American Society for Information Science*, Vol. 26, No. 5: 271-279.

23. Taha, H. A. (2007). *Operations research: an introduction*. New Delhi: Prentice-Hall of India.

24. Thomas, P. A. and Robertson, S. E. (1975). A Computer Simulation Model of Library Operations. *Journal of Documentation*, Vol. 31, No. 1: 1-18.

25. Ven et al. (2008). Stimulating information sharing, collaboration and learning in operations research with libOR. *International Journal on Digital Libraries*, Vol. 8, No. 2: 79-90.

26. Warwick, J. (2009). On the future of library operations research. *Library Management*, Vol. 30, No. 3: 176-184.

27. Warwick, J. and Bell, G. (2009). A Framework for Exploring Organizational Learning in the Academic Library. *Library & Information Research*, Vol. 33, No. 103: 16-31.

28. Yu, G.; Li, Y. and Yu, D. (2009). Simulation study of the inventory effect of the scientific paper publishing process. *Journal of Information Science*, Vol. 35, No. 4: 414-425.

6.2. CONSULTED WORKS

1. Bärwolff, M. (2006). Tight prior open source equilibrium: The rise of open source as a source of economic welfare. *First Monday*, Vol. 11, No. 1. Available at: *http://firstmonday.org/htbin/cgiwrap/bin/ojs/index.php/fm/article/view/1309/1229*

2. Bellassai, M. C. (1983). *Survey of Federal libraries, fiscal year 1978*. Washington DC: King Research, Inc.

3. Duff, M. J. B. (1983). Neighbourhood Operators. In:

O. J. Braddick and A. C. Sleigh (Eds.), *Physical and Biological Processing of Images*. Berlin: Springer.

4. Fichter, D. (2004). Heuristic and Cognitive Walk-Through Evaluations. *Online*, Vol. 28, No. 3: 53-56.

5. Fidczuk, R.; Beebe, L. and Wallas, P. (2007). Today's Journal Cost: Print vs. Online. *Serials Librarian*, Vol. 52, No. 3/4: 341-348.

6. Fiet, J.; Norton, W. I. and Clouse, V. G. H. (2007). Systematic search as a source of technical innovation: An empirical test. *Journal of Engineering & Technology Management*, Vol. 24, No. 4: 329-346.

7. Gackowski, Z. J. (2005). Informing Systems in Business Environments: A Purpose-Focused View. *Informing Science*, Vol. 8: 101-122.

8. Gallant, L. M.; Boone, G. M. and Heap, A. (2007). Five heuristics for designing and evaluating Web-based communities. *First Monday*, Vol. 12, No. 3. Available at: *http://firstmonday.org/htbin/cgiwrap/bin/ojs/index.php/fm/article/view/1626/1541*

9. Georgantzas, N. C. and Kalsamakas, E. (2007). Disruptive Innovation Strategy Effects on Hard-Disk Maker Population: A System Dynamics Study. *Information Resources Management Journal*, Vol. 20, No. 2: 90-107.

10. Gerlich, B. and Whatley, E. (2009). Using the READ Scale for Staffing Strategies: The Georgia College and State University Experience. *Library Leadership & Management*, Vol. 23, No. 1: 26-30.

11. Harris, B. R. (2006). Visual information literacy via

visual means: three heuristics. *Reference Services Review*, Vol. 34, No. 2: 213-221.

12. Hirshon, A. (1986). *Automated library systems in ARL Libraries*. Washington DC: Association of Research Libraries.

13. Holte, R. C.; Felner, A.; Newton, J.; Meshulam, R. and Furcy, D. (2006). Maximizing over multiple pattern databases speeds up heuristic search. *Artificial Intelligence*, Vol. 170, No. 16/17: 1123-1136.

14. Jiang, J. and Zhai, C. (2007). An empirical study of tokenization strategies for biomedical information retrieval. *Information Retrieval*, Vol. 10, No. 4/5: 341-363.

15. Jolly, R. and Wakeland, W. (2009). Using Agent Based Simulation and Game Theory Analysis to Study Knowledge Flow in Organizations: The KMscape. *International Journal of Knowledge Management*, Vol. 5, No. 1: 17-28.

16. Kang, I.; Na, S.; Lee, S.; Jung, H.; Kim, P.; Sung, W. and Lee, J. (2009). On co-authorship for author disambiguation. *Information Processing & Management*, Vol. 45, No. 1: 84-97.

17. McCain, K. W. (1988). Evaluating Cocited Author Search Performance in a Collaborative Specialty. *Journal of the American Society for Information Science*, Vol. 39, No. 6: 428-431.

18. Mora, M.; Gelman, O.; Forgionne, G.; Petkov, D. and Cano, J. (2007). Integrating the Fragmented Pieces of IS Research Paradigms and Frameworks: A Systems Approach. *Information Resources*

Management Journal, Vol. 20, No. 2: 1-22.

19. Mustafa, S. H. (2005). Word-oriented approximate string matching using occurrence heuristic tables: A heuristic for searching Arabic text. *Journal of the American Society for Information Science & Technology*, Vol. 56, No. 14: 1504-1511.

20. Newman, D. J. and Block, S. (2006). Probabilistic topic decomposition of an eighteenth-century American newspaper. *Journal of the American Society for Information Science & Technology*, Vol. 57, No. 6: 753-767.

21. Rada, R. and Bicknell, E. (1989). Ranking Documents with a Thesaurus. *Journal of the American Society for Information Science*, Vol. 40, No. 5: 304-310.

22. Spindler, T. (2009). Statistical Analysis Models: Applications for Libraries. *Library Leadership & Management*, Vol. 23, No. 1: 12-16.

23. Varadarajan, R.; Hristidis, V. and Li, T. (2006). Searching the Web Using Composed Pages. *SIGIR Forum*, Vol. 39: 713-714.

24. Vigeannel-Larive, O. (2002). La bibliothèque, laboratoire du mathématicien. *Bulletin des Biblioteques de France*, Vol. 47, No. 6: 50-54.

25. Yang, C. C. and Li, K. W. (2005). A heuristic method based on a statistical approach for Chinese text segmentation. *Journal of the American Society for Information Science & Technology*, Vol. 56, No. 13: 1438-1447.

26. Ylikoski, T. (2005). A sequence analysis of consumers'

online searches. *Internet Research*, Vol. 15, No. 2: 181-194.

6.3. FURTHER READINGS

1. Adeyemi, N. M. (1977). Library operations research-purpose, tools, utility, and implications for developing libraries. *Libri*, Vol. 27, No. 1: 22-30.

2. Amick, D. J. (1970). A Multivariate Statistical Analysis of the Use of a Scientific Computer Based Current-Awareness Information Retrieval System. *Journal of the American Society for Information Science*, Vol. 21, No. 3: 171-178.

3. Bookstein, A. (1974). Allocation of Resources in an Information System. *Journal of the American Society for Information Science*, Vol. 25, No. 1: 52-58.

4. Buckland, M. K. (1972). An Operations Research Study of a Variable Loan and Duplication Policy at the University of Lancaster. *The Library Quarterly*, Vol. 42, No. 1: 97–106.

5. Chen, C. C. (1976). *Applications of Operations Research Models to Libraries: A Case Study of the Use of Monographs in the Francis A. Countway Library of Medicine, Harvard University*. Cambridge, Mass: MIT Press.

6. Dahlin, T. C. (1991). Operations research and organizational decision-making in academic libraries. *Collection Management*, Vol. 14, No. 3/4: 49-60.

7. Dobson, P.; Myles, J. and Jackson, P. (2007). Making the Case for Critical Realism: Examining the Implementation of Automated Performance

Management Systems. *Information Resources Management Journal*, Vol. 20, No. 2: 138-152.

8. Elton, M. and Vickery, B. (1973). The scope of operational research in the library and information field. *Aslib Proceedings*, Vol. 25, No. 8: 305-319.

9. Gelman, E. and Sichel, H. S. (1987). Library Book Circulation and the Beta-Binomial Distribution. *Journal of the American Society for Information Science*, Vol. 38, No. 1: 4-12.

10. Goyal, S. K. (1970). Application of operations research to problems of determining appropriate loan periods for periodicals. *Libri*, Vol. 20, No. 1: 94-100.

11. Goyal, S. K. (1973). Allocation of Library Funds to Different Departments of a University-An Operational Research Approach. *College and Research Libraries*, Vol. 34, No. 3: 219-222.

12. Grant, R. S. (1971). Predicting the Need for Multiple Copies of Books. *Journal of Library Automation*, Vol. 4, No. 2: 64-71.

13. Gupta, S. M. and Ravindram, A. (1974). Optimal Storage of Books by Size: An Operations Research Approach. *Journal of the American Society for Information Science*, Vol. 25, No. 6: 354-357.

14. Hamill, K. A. and Zamora, A. (1980). The Use of Titles for Automatic Document Classification. *Journal of the American Society for Information Science*, Vol. 31, No. 6: 396-402.

15. Kantor, P. (1979). Review of Library Operations Research. *Library Resources*, Vol. 1, No. 4: 295-345.

16. Kraft, D. H. and Liesener, J. W. (1979). Planning and Budgeting for School Media Programs at the Building, District, and Regional Levels: O.R. in the Little Red Schoolhouse. *Journal of the American Society for Information Science*, Vol. 30, No. 1: 41-50.

17. Kraft, D. H. and McDonald, D. D. (1976). Library Operations Research: Its Past and Our Future. In *The Information Age*, D. P. Hammer (Ed.). Metuchen, New Jersey: Scarecrow Press, 122-144.

18. Kwok, K. L. (1985). A Probabilistic Theory of Indexing and Similarity Measure Based on Cited and Citing Documents. *Journal of the American Society for Information Science*, Vol. 36, No. 5: 342-351.

19. Leimkuhler, F. F. (1968). Mathematical Models for Library Systems Analysis. *Drexel Library Quarterly*, Vol. 4, No. 3: 185-196.

20. Leimkuhler, F. F. (1970). Library Operations Research: An Engineering Approach to Information Problems. *Engineering Education*, Vol. 60: 363-365.

21. Leimkuhler, F. F. (1977). Operational Analysis of Library Systems. *Information Processing and Management*, Vol. 13, No. 2: 79-93.

22. Leimkuhler, F. F. and Cooper, M. D. (1971). Analytical Models for Library Planning. *Journal of the American Society for Information Science*, Vol. 22, No. 6: 390-398.

23. Magrath, L. L. (1982). Computers in the library. The human element. *Information Technology & Libraries*, Vol. 1, No. 3: 266-270.

24. Mansfield, U. (1982). The Systems Movement: An Overview for Information Scientists. *Journal of the American Society for Information Science*, Vol. 33, No. 6: 375-382.

25. Mcclure, C. R. (1977). Linear Programming and Library Delivery Systems. *Library Resources and Technical Services*, Vol. 21, No. 4: 333-344.

26. Min, H. (1988). The Dynamic Expansion and Relocation of Capacitated Public Facilities: A Multi-Objective Approach. *Computer and Operations Research*, Vol. 15, No. 3: 243-252.

27. Morse, P. M. (1968). *Library Effectiveness: A Systems Approach*. Cambridge, Mass: MIT Press.

28. Morse, P. M. (1970). Search Theory and Browsing. *The Library Quarterly*, Vol. 40, No. 4: 391-408.

29. Morse, P. M. (1972). Measures of Library Effectiveness. *The Library Quarterly*, Vol. 42, No. 1: 15-30.

30. Pitt, W. B. and Kraft, D. H. (1974). Buy or Copy? A Library Operations Research Model. *Information Storage and Retrieval*, Vol. 10, No. 9-10: 331-341.

31. Schniederjans, M. and Santhanam, R. (1989). A Zero-One Goal Programming Approach for the Journal Selection and Cancellation Problem. *Computer and Operations Research*, Vol. 16, No. 6: 557-565.

32. Segars, A. H. and Grover, V. (1998). Strategic information systems planning success: an investigation of the construct and its measurement. *MIS Quarterly*, Vol. 22, No. 2: 139-163.

33. Slamecka, V. (1972). A Selective Bibliography on Library Operations Research. *The Library Quarterly*, Vol. 42, No. 1: 152-158.

34. Stephenson, S. V. and Sage, A, P. (2007). Information and Knowledge Perspectives in Systems Engineering and Management for Innovation and Productivity through Enterprise Resource Planning. *Information Resources Management Journal*, Vol. 20, No. 2: 44-73.

35. Taylor, R. G. (1987). Determining the Minimum Number of Online Terminals Needed to Meet Various Library Service Policies. *Information Technology and Libraries*, Vol. 6, No. 3: 197-204.

36. Taylor, R. G. (1988). Measures of Expected Online Catalog Performance for Public Access Terminals. *Information Technology and Libraries*, Vol. 7, No. 1: 24-29.

37. Vertinsky, I. (1984). INFOR special issue on information processing and decision making in situations involving risks. *INFOR*, Vol. 22, No. 2: 79-79.

38. Warwick, J. P. (1993). Predicting user behaviour in academic libraries: a contribution from operational research. *Collection Management*, Vol. 17, No. 4: 1-10.

39. Williams, R F. (1985). The complete operations research analyst. *Proceedings of the Conference on the Simulation Profession*, 29-34.

40. Wright, K. C. (1971). Assured Failure in Information Center Operations. *Journal of the American Society for Information Science*, Vol. 22, No. 4: 294-295.

41. Yovlts, M. C. and Foulk, C. R. (1985). Experiments and Analysis of Information Use and Value In a Decision-Making Context. *Journal of the American Society for Information Science*, Vol. 36, No. 2: 63-81.

Index